THE JEWISH RELIGION
IN THE TIME OF JESUS

The Jewish Religion in the Time of Jesus

BY

G. HOLLMAN

OF HALLE

TRANSLATED BY EDWARD LUMMIS, M. A.

BOSTON
AMERICAN UNITARIAN ASSOCIATION
1909

PREFACE

THE account given in the following pages is intended to make accessible to all who are interested in the subject the present state of investigation in this field, as it is exhibited especially in the great works of Schürer and Bousset. While its purpose is to furnish the lay reader with an introductory guide, the more instructed will perhaps find it not unwelcome as a brief survey of the subject. Considering the uncertainty and obscurity in which, in spite of all the labours of the last ten years, later Judaism is still involved, I have aimed not so much at completeness, as to bring out sharply and clearly the decisive and fundamental lines. I have intentionally dealt somewhat more fully with the Jewish apocalyptic, because it is least known to the lay reader, because a popular account of it has not yet appeared, and because it is precisely on this ground that so many preconditions for understanding the thought-world of Jesus, in the light of religious history, are to be found. I recommend all those to whom post-exilic Judaism is still entirely unknown to read the Appendix first, so as to acquire at least some of the elementary facts necessary to the understanding of the historical situation.

GEORG HOLLMANN.

HALLE, 15 *December*, 1904.

CONTENTS

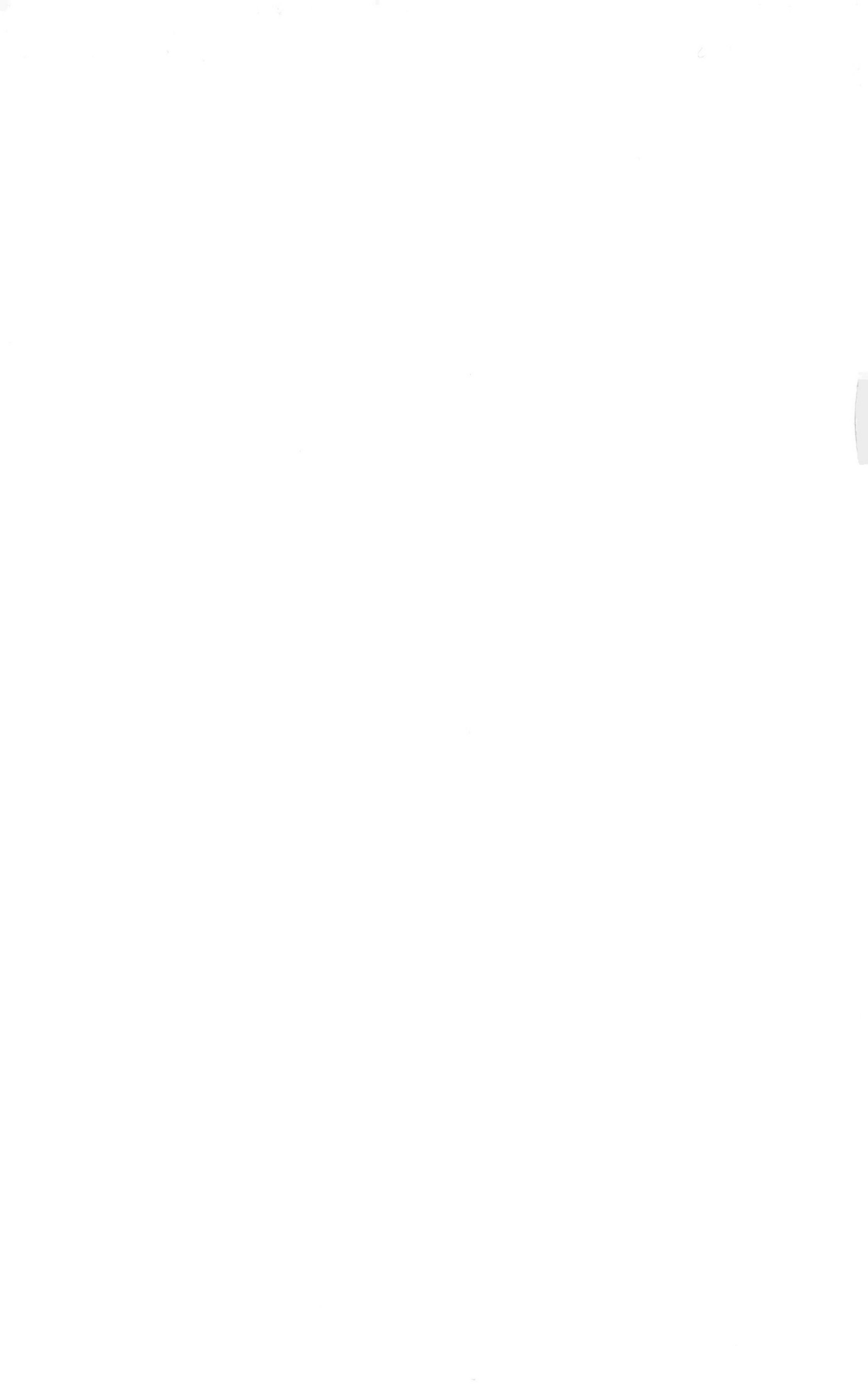

INTRODUCTION

WHAT was the religion of the Jews at the time of Jesus' public work? This is not merely a question for the scholar who happens to take an interest in this special religion at a definite date in its development; it is of the widest possible significance. Every one who wishes to understand Jesus, or Paul, or early Christianity in general, must find an answer to it; for the new religion took its rise in the bosom of Judaism, bears the tokens of its origin, and had to struggle upwards through severe contests into freedom. Only he who is able to believe that Christianity suddenly descended, a perfectly new thing, from a supernatural world into this, can remain indifferent to the surroundings in which it arose. The rest of us must take account of the general law of origins —that every new manifestation, without prejudice to its originality, is conditioned, among other things, by the environment in which it arose. Even Jesus is subject to this law. In spite of all efforts to Aryanise him the fact remains that he can only be comprehended by means of Judaism. His conception of the universe has its roots in Judaism. This is the foundation on which all the mighty freshness of his moral and religious personality is based. For this reason all who wish to understand the religion of Jesus must also know the religion which the Jews had at the time of his appearance.

Is it enough if we read the Old Testament? Certainly not. That was the serious mistake made by a bygone period, an unhistorical type of thought. The Old Testament could not possibly suffice for our purpose unless its writings came down to the time of Jesus, so that we might really discern in them the religion of the Jews who were then alive. But that is not the case. Most of the Old Testament writings are very considerably older. The books which belong for certain to the two centuries before Christ are only a few Psalms, Daniel and Esther, with perhaps Ecclesiastes. Since the time of the Maccabees, which marks the great turning-point in the post-exile period, the

Jewish religion had undergone a very important development; this is easily perceived when we examine the pieces of Jewish literature which stand nearest to the time of Jesus. A distinction must be made between the religion of the Jews of the time of Christ, and the deposit of a long process of religious development, such as lies before us in the Old Testament. This appears to be a very simple truth; but hard fighting has been needed to establish it, and there are many who do not understand it even now.

The recognition of this truth does not in the least imply a depreciation of the Old Testament. A knowledge of its contents, indeed, is quite indispensable to the study of the Jewish religion in Jesus' time. It was the Bible of the Jews of that age, and seemed to them to contain merely their own religion. The Old Testament was always their base and starting-point, but it must be owned that they had gone, unconsciously, very far beyond it. Still the holy Scripture served also as a counterpoise to the new religious development. Should the religious sense be offended by any of the elements of the religion which prevailed in its own time, it was enabled to survey past ages, and to recover better things which had been left behind. Jesus it was, pre-eminently Jesus, who often reached back beyond the religion of Jewry to the religion of Israel, especially that of its prophets. But, after all, the literature which will be of first importance in our study of the Jewish religion in Jesus' time is the religious literature which that time itself produced.

CHAPTER I

UNITY OF THE CHURCH AND DISTINCTIONS WITHIN IT

WHEN Jesus appeared the Jewish nation was not one of those numerous Asiatic races about which people neither knew nor cared. On the contrary, it was spread over the whole world, as every one knows from the story of Pentecost.[1] Greeks and Romans, learned and lewd, all knew the Jews from their own point of view, and had their own dealings with them. We have many testimonies of heathen writers to prove this. Judaism had become a world-wide power. Important beginnings had been made, especially in Egypt, before the Maccabean age; but the extension of Judaism in the grand sense does not seem to have originated until after the great upheaval of the people in the war of liberation

[1] Acts 2^{9-11}.

under the Maccabees. The racial forces then set free sought for opportunities of exercise, both within and beyond the land of Palestine. The Herodian age in particular, because of the sagacious pro-Roman policy of the Idumeans, may well have been favourable to the diffusion of the Jews throughout the entire Roman empire. And with regard to the time of the Emperor Augustus, in which Jesus was born, Strabo is able to write about the Jews: 'They are spread about in almost every city of the globe, and it is not easy to find any place in the world which has not given shelter to this people, and does not stand under its sway.'[1] They were remarkably strongly represented in Egypt and Cyrene, and in cosmopolitan cities like Rome and Alexandria. The question forcibly suggests itself—what was it that connected the Jews in foreign lands with their native Palestine? What common bond united them all?

It was not the bond of nationality. No doubt the foreign Jews always felt that they were Jews. But such a tie will not long endure unless, over and above the racial idiosyncrasy—which is,

[1] According to Josephus, Antiquities 14, 7².

beyond question, especially sharp and strong among the Jews,—there is a strong, imposing, independent mother country, whose far-off scions can think of her with pride and joy as still their own, and gain from her the power to preserve their national feeling. But what was Palestine in the Augustan age? A subject-state of Rome. Since the Babylonian captivity the Jewish people had never been able to regain any lasting national independence.[1] It had been tossed from hand to hand, from Persian to Macedonian, from Egyptian to Syrian, only to rest caught at last in the brazen clasp of Rome. But a subject-people cannot keep its distant members for ever, if the question is to be decided by national feeling. There certainly were times when the ancient national force broke out with an almost volcanic, unearthly fury. One such outbreak occurred when the Syrian ruler Antiochus Epiphanes tried, with brutal violence, to force the Jewish people to accept Grecian culture. The bloody struggles under the leadership of the Maccabees, which gave answer to this attempt, meant first of all a passionate flaming up of the old national

[1] Except during the Hasmonean dynasty, 141–63 B.C.

strength; and their immediate consequence was a ruthless exclusiveness against everything foreign,[1] a hardening of national peculiarities, a burning concern for national independence. And again, just at the time of Jesus' appearance and in the next few decades, an extraordinary political fermentation was at work in the Jewish people. The yoke of Roman rule was growing intolerable. The stronger the feeling that they had fallen under the sceptre of an impregnable, universal power, so much the more convulsive, we may even say feverish, grew the longing for their ancient freedom. 'Freedom from Rome at any price' was the watchword of the people. Insurrection blazed forth now here, now there; false Messiahs multiplied, promising the deluded populace that they would restore the kingdom of David in greater glory than of old; until that last great rising came in the seventh decade of the first century, that mad, hopeless struggle with an irresistible antagonist, which ended in the overwhelming catastrophe of the year 70 A.D. These were certainly last attempts of the Jews, attempts which will always command our sympathy, to maintain them-

[1] The book of Esther is a striking testimony to this.

selves as a nation. But they cannot blind us to the fact that, in spite of all that tense national feeling, the tie which united all Jews was not nationality. A decisive proof of this is the incontestable fact that Judaism not only survived the final collapse of the nation, which began in the year 70 with the destruction of Jerusalem and ended with the suppression of the insurrection of Barcochba in 135, but did so with ease, without its existence being threatened for a single moment. It must therefore have been something other than national community that held the Jews together amid all their dispersion, amid all their restless wandering, and indeed has held them together from that time down to the present day.

Imperceptibly—one might almost say by stealth—a yet stronger bond, a spiritual bond, had been woven, the unity of one common Church. Whether the Jew was in Rome, Corinth, or Alexandria, everywhere he found his synagogue, his Bible, his feasts, above all his Sabbath, and the contribution to the Temple in Jerusalem; everywhere the same spiritual atmosphere, the air of one and the same Church. In this connexion the synagogue must first be mentioned.

The focus of the religious life of the Jews was no longer the Temple of Jerusalem. They yielded to it, indeed, the due respect and reverence which was a tradition from their fathers. Every year the Temple tribute was collected throughout the Diaspora[1]; every one must pay it from his twentieth year onwards, and no true Jew shirked the duty. Enormous sums, carried by accredited ambassadors, flowed in this way into the sanctuary. Moreover pilgrimages were paid every year to Jerusalem, the holy city, and its Temple, just as later the Mohammedans went as pilgrims to Mecca. Nevertheless it was inevitable that the importance of the Temple should decline, as it actually did. If even the Galilean found great difficulty in journeying to Jerusalem, how much greater must have been the difficulties of the Jews of the Diaspora, who dwelt at remote distances. There must certainly have been many to whom it was impossible, for reasons of money or health, to come even once a year to Jerusalem. And what signifies after all one single festal visit to the holy site? The religious life cannot be nourished on

[1] *Diaspora* means Dispersion, to wit that of the Jews in the world outside Palestine.

that the whole year through. In this case, too, a decisive proof that Jewish piety, in spite of its external reverence towards the Temple worship, had been imperceptibly detached from it, lies in the fact that the destruction of the sanctuary and its worship in the year 70 did not seriously impair the strength of Judaism.

The actual religious life had long before found its new focus in the synagogue, an institution which has lasted to the present day, weathered all storms, and so proved its utility. The word synagogue, i.e. 'assembly,' denotes both the religious community and the place in which the inhabitants of any district assemble for divine service on Sabbath, feast-days, and fast-days.[1] It cannot now be determined with any certainty when the first synagogues were established.

[1] The chief religious festivals of the Jews, besides the Sabbath, are: the Passover (at the end of March or beginning of April; a memorial of the Exodus from Egypt), the Feast of Weeks or of First-fruits (about Whitsuntide, the festival of the first harvest and of the Law), the great Feast of Atonement (at the end of September, expiation for the whole people), the Feast of Booths (at the end of September and beginning of October, the festival of the second harvest and a memorial of the forty years in the wilderness), the Feast of Purim (at the end of February or the beginning of March; cf. the book of Esther).

Whether they were first used during the Exile, or immediately afterwards, or on the other hand not until after the time of the Maccabees, is still a controverted question. It is enough for us that at the time of Jesus' appearance the synagogue and the Sabbath services were perfectly settled institutions. As regards the procedure in worship we shall go into greater detail in our next chapter. At present the important point is to make clear the way in which these synagogues, which existed in all Jewish communities, with their similar services, were certain to make for the union of the dispersed members of the Jewish nation, wherever they might be.

In the synagogue the Jew found his Bible, the Old Testament.

The collection, which had grown gradually in the post-exilic age, was closed as regards its main contents about the year 130, as we know from the Prologue to the work of Jesus ben Sirach. Of its three parts, the Law, the Prophets, the Hagiographa, i.e. sacred writings, or K'thuvim, i.e. writings, the third alone was still an uncertain quantity in the time of Jesus. This may easily be perceived in the fact that in the New Testament the writings of the Old Testament are usually spoken of as 'Law,' or 'Law and Prophets.'[1] Several of the Hagiographa, for instance the book of Koheleth or the Preacher, seem to have been matters of dispute among the contemporaries of Jesus. The limits of the canon were not set with absolute certainty until the end of the first Christian century. The fact that various additions to it were to be found among the Jews of Alexandria is not of any considerable significance. The part which was most important for the religious life, the Law, and alongside that the Prophets, were found by the Jew everywhere, in the Greek version of Alexandria, known as the Septuagint. It was so called because, according to the legend, it had been translated by seventy-two learned Jews in an identical wording, although each had worked apart. Hebrew was now understood only by the learned; the ordinary tongue used in Palestine was Syrian; otherwise Greek was spoken. These Biblical writings, and above all the Law, had the highest authority. Every word was decisive. The doctrine of Inspiration

[1] An exception occurs in Luke 24^{27}, where the Alexandrian division is followed.

was formed. God had intimated to the authors through his spirit not merely the matter, but even the very wording. This idea took an especially violent form in Alexandrian Judaism, where the conception had actually been reached which represents the sacred writer as a mere speaking-tube or pen-holder of the holy spirit. It was extended to the Greek translation.

And this word of God was read every Sabbath day, section by section, in the synagogue. By means of this Bible the young life was trained in the schools, since school teaching meant essentially instruction in the Bible, together with the learning of prayers by heart. In the time of Jesus well-ordered boys' schools may already have been found, not only in the chief towns. Jesus himself gives us the decided impression that he had known his Bible well from schooldays onwards. Knowledge of the Bible and loyalty to the Bible was the mark of the pious as well as of the cultured Jew. How strong was the bond of union which the nation possessed in this book!

On the other hand we cannot speak of any fixed dogma in the time of Jesus. There was, no doubt, a general fundamental conviction that the observance of the Law was necessary to the attainment of salvation, but it had not been dogmatically formulated. If anything could be styled a fixed Jewish dogma, it would be monotheism, the belief in one God. In the 'Shepherd of Hermas,' which in many respects betrays a Jewish influence, we read, 'Before all things believe that God is one.'[1] In Palestine such a belief was a matter of course; but the Jews of the Diaspora, amid their Pagan surroundings, learned to realize in quite a new way the immense importance of this one article of faith, so that its counterpart, a belief in the satanic and demoniac origin of Pagan idolatry, became equally firmly established. The time when a Resurrection dogma might have been spoken of had already gone by. In the Judaism of Palestine, indeed, and in extensive circles in the Diaspora, it could still be maintained, but the Judaism of Alexandria, through the mouth of weighty representatives, had rejected the Resurrection. More might be said for a dogma of Retribution, since all the late Jewish writings, except Ecclesiastes, are at one in teaching Retribution after death. Finally it must be pointed out

[1] Hermas, Commandments, I, 1.

that the Jewish Church, in contrast, for instance, with the Christian Catholic Church, possessed no sacraments which guarantee salvation, and indeed no guarantee of any sort except the one. Everybody must fulfil the Law for himself, and sacrifice can only redeem certain definite derelictions. The solitary exception which might be adduced is the doctrine of propitiation through suffering, and especially through the death of the righteous and of martyrs, who had played so great a part since the time of the Maccabees[1]; but it is doubtful how far this doctrine was known or accepted in the time of Jesus. The process by which it afterwards assumed great importance was then only beginning.[2]

But the most striking evidence of the force with which the Jewish people itself felt its unity as a Church is the movement towards propaganda, towards the dissemination of the Jewish religion among the Gentiles, a movement which was at work not only in the Diaspora, but also—if not with equal strength—in Palestine. It was an

[1] Cf. their remarkable prominence in the Revelation of John, 6^{9-11}, 12^{11}, 14^{13}, etc.

[2] The only passages which come into account are II Macc. 7^{37}, IV Macc. 6^{29}, 17^{22}.

outcome of their common and well-founded sense of the religious and moral superiority of Judaism to the whole of Paganism, even to the renowned Hellenistic culture. The Jew has something better than any heathen sage has ever offered, a pure faith in God, an earnest and strict morality. Unfortunately this just conviction often made use, in the literary propaganda, of very reprehensible methods. The Greek writers of the past, poets, philosophers, and historians, were made, in a whole series of coarse forgeries, to bear testimony to the truths of the Jewish faith. What an effect it must have if the Jewish religion was glorified in verses of the divine Homer or of Hesiod, if even ancient historians had drawn attention to this incomparable people! Above all the Greek philosopher of widest influence, the great Plato, was pressed into the cause. The Jews did not shrink from representing him, together with Heraclitus, Pythagoras, and others, as a disciple of Moses, and they maintained in all seriousness that Greek philosophy had received its best strength from the Jewish religion. In order to understand these strange doings we must always hold in mind the impression, from which the Jew could never free himself, that the loftiest utterances of Greek philosophers about God and morality were to be found in his own religion in greater clearness and certainty, surrounded with the sheen of divine revelation. They seemed to him but a weak echo of the pristine diapason. And this not merely assumed but real superiority of the Jewish religion and morality had a mighty effect upon others. It was met on the Pagan side by the stronger and stronger longing of expiring Antiquity for religious satisfaction, the hunger for revelation, true, certain, divine revelation. What a great work of preparation had been done by the post-Aristotelean philosophy, with its ever-increasing interest in religious problems! What utter disintegration had befallen the old, naive, popular conceptions! What an effect the Greek translation of the Old Testament must have had, by means of which it was possible to gain a real insight into the ancient, sacred literature of the Jews! As a result of all this the Jewish propaganda met with a remarkable welcome. Wherever there were Jewish communities a circle of adherents, especially women, soon clustered around them. Philo says of the Jewish Law, 'It attracts and converts all, barbarians and Greeks, dwellers on the continent and islanders, races of the East and the West, Europeans, Asiatics, the whole inhabited world from one end to the other.' The new adherents were called 'proselytes'—literally, 'new-comers.'

The current distinction which we learned at school between 'Proselytes of the Gate' and 'Proselytes of Righteousness'[1] did not arise until much later, and has nothing to do with another distinction, which must be recognized in the time of Jesus. The Proselytes were those Gentiles who received circumcision, underwent a purificatory immersion and made a propitiatory sacrifice, and in this way actually became Jews. They can never have been very numerous. We must distinguish from them another class, 'those that feared God,' that is to say those Gentiles who attended the synagogue, accepted monotheism, and also observed certain parts of the Law, such as the command of the Sabbath. They existed in great numbers, and formed the chief result of the Jewish propaganda. At this point

[1] Aliens resident in Palestine; and Gentiles who had become Jews.

we must at least refer to the enormous importance of these 'God-fearing' people for the Christian mission. Paul, on his missionary journeys, made true disciples among those adherents of Judaism. They prepared a fostering soil for Christian ideas. And these 'God-fearing' men had not those obstinate prejudices which characterized the Jews. The extent to which the missionary movement was astir even amid the Judaism of Palestine at that time is evinced by the saying of Jesus, that the Pharisees compassed sea and land to make one proselyte.[1] This movement towards expansion was at length crippled by the growth of fanaticism hostile to Rome, and finally by the unrestrained bitterness of feeling which prevailed after the fall of Jerusalem.

By this propaganda, together with the exclusiveness of the Jews and their claim to religious and moral superiority, that anti-Semitic feeling was engendered which deepened into passionate persecutions of the Jews, and is well known to us in Greek and Roman writers. Tacitus has given us a celebrated picture of the Jews in the fifth book of his History. He depicts them indeed as the

[1] Matt. 23[15].

most repulsive race, the most despicable section of the subjugated peoples, and throughout all his remarks there breathes such a note of disdain that they give us the best possible measure of the embittered feeling of that age. Judaism was actually felt as a dangerous power. But amid it all we can clearly perceive the impression from which even the Gentiles could not escape, that in spite of its dispersion over the globe the Jewish people formed a spiritual unity, which pressed victoriously forward.

Up to this point we have fixed our regard exclusively upon the factors which prove the ecclesiastical unity of the Judaism of that time. Nevertheless we may take it for granted that here, as everywhere in life, we shall find certain differences within the unity itself.

We have already had occasion to hint at differences between the Jews in and outside Palestine, with reference, for instance, to belief in the Resurrection. Now we must lay direct emphasis on the fact that considerable divergences from the Judaism of Palestine were developed among the Jews of the Diaspora, not merely on their whole outer mode of life—as in constant intercourse with Gentiles, exclusive use of the Greek language, preponderance of the mercantile profession—but also in religion. Much of what was still in full vigour in Palestine had perforce, amid heathen surroundings, to give way—regulations of the Law, requirements of worship, part of which, such as a number of precepts concerning purification, could only be carried out when the Temple was accessible. Some elements, again, which existed in Palestine, came out into special prominence through contrast with an utterly dissimilar environment—for instance, monotheism and the moral demands. In this way, gently and insensibly, there came to pass a remarkable simplification of the religion. The legal and ceremonial part was not indeed disavowed, but its demands on a number of matters necessarily fell into the background, while the numerous separate religious conceptions tended to crystallize around certain prominent points. It is obvious that the Jews outside Palestine were much more exposed to foreign influences than those of Palestine. Nevertheless these Jews of the Diaspora remained Jews, felt themselves to be Jews, strictly observed the ceremonial law, kept their Sabbath and their feasts. So far as we know there was only one point in the Diaspora, Alexandria, where the difference grew really deep. The fourth book of the Maccabees, the Wisdom of Solomon, Aristobulus, and, above all, Philo show us that there were circles among the Alexandrian Jews which had entered into so close an alliance with Greek culture that we often do not know whether we are dealing with Jews or Greeks. True, even a man like Philo did not wish to be anything but a Jew; his philosophy takes the form of an explanation of the Mosaic law; but it really was something new, an attempt to unite Jewish religion and Greek culture, which did not do justice to either. It is not our task to deal more closely with these Alexandrian Jews and their views. That has been done in another book in this series.[1] They do not concern the religion with which Jesus came in contact. It is possible, to me it seems even probable, that through their means Greek thoughts occasionally percolated through to the Jews in Palestine, but this process cannot be certainly traced. It is conceivable, for instance, that Jesus'

[1] 'The Preparation for Christianity in Greek Philosophy,' by Prof. Pfleiderer, pp. 60–66.

saying, 'God alone is good,'[1] was connected in this way with the Greek idea of God as the highest perfection. But on such points we cannot be certain. On the whole it cannot be shown that Alexandria influenced Jesus; it was afterwards, on the other hand, of world-wide importance in the development of Christian theology.

If we turn our gaze upon the Judaism of Palestine, which, besides being the only Judaism which affects Jesus, was also the real centre of gravity of the Jewish religion, we find here also a number of distinctions which must be recognized. The circles which dominate the religious and ecclesiastical life are not, as might have been expected, the priests, but the theologians: for that, more than anything else, is what the 'scribes' are. A learned acquaintance with the Mosaic law is their profession. But since the Law is also the book of ordinary jurisprudence these men are also the jurists, the lawyers of their time. It is true that the Law, in this sense, was to be found in the five books of Moses, but it must be applied to the needs of the present time; and this opened out a rich field of work for learned acumen. In

[1] Mark 10[18].

this way through the labours of the scribes there was gradually formed a new customary law alongside the written Law, the so-called *Halacha*, 'what is usual.' This new tradition professed to be no more than an exposition and application of the letter of the Law, an exposition for which quite definite rules, formulated by the scribe Hillel, were introduced. But in reality it was an extension of the Law, such as tended more and more to thrust the scripture itself into the background, and was of the highest importance, because it kept touch with the requirements of practical life. At first a merely oral tradition, it was afterwards reduced to writing; the fact that it was said to have been handed down from the time of Moses is the clearest evidence of the high value ascribed to it. Since the scribes were chained to the sacred text, they always laboured under a certain constraint, which could only be overcome by the most arbitrary methods of exegesis. Those parts of the Old Testament which are not of a legal character were more freely worked over; the scribes simply read into the text what the views of a later age demanded. For instance, the course of past history was depicted as, according to present ideas, it ought to have run; an excellent example of this method is to be found within the Old Testament itself, in the two books of the Chronicles, as compared with the books of Samuel. The moral and religious utterances of the sacred scripture were treated in the same way. They were twisted or supplemented until they conformed to modern conceptions. The whole of this transformation and adornment of the non-legal parts of scripture was called *Haggada*, 'narration.' By means of this *Mishna*—literally 'repetition,' in the sense of 'teaching'—as set forth in the *Halacha* and *Haggada*, the customary law and the new, imaginative narration, the Old Testament was more and more thickly overgrown with the creeping plants of tradition and human ordinances. A fateful development! The piety which was built upon this tradition could not escape being as artificial, mechanical, fantastic, and often puerile as its foundation. Jesus felt this very clearly, and expressed himself with extreme severity against the tradition: 'Right well do you repudiate the commandment of God, to keep your own tradition.'[1]

[1] Mark 7^{9}; the whole section, 7^{1-15}, should be read.

The guardians of this portentous growth were the scribes; and at the time of Jesus' appearance their influence dominated the people at all points.

This was the outcome of a long historical process. In the post-exilic Jewish community, at the beginning of which the learning of Ezra stands prominently forth, piety and wisdom had gradually become merged and confounded. The 'pious sage' displaced the prophet. The more definitely post-exilic Judaism, which gathered about the Law, became a book-religion, the greater the importance which the learned man, the sage, must gain. And even though in the sayings of Jesus, son of Sirach, this wisdom still showed a free outlook and wide horizon, it was inevitable that it should grow narrower and narrower. In the time of Jesus the man who knows the Law is the only true sage. From the close of the Maccabean period particular names among these scribes begin to stand out more clearly. The most renowned are Hillel and Shammai, heads of contrasted schools, and contemporaries of Jesus. The differences between the two are by no means formidable; they have to do with trifles, which seem to us ridiculous—for instance, the question whether on a feast-day a ladder, which is leaning against a dovecot, may be carried across to another dovecot —but they show into what dreariness and deadness a religion under such leadership must fall, how the life of it must simply be crushed out. Hillel was, on the whole, the milder of the two; he also advocated the mission to the Gentiles; Shammai was more severe. Besides these two the teacher of the apostle Paul, Gamaliel, is especially well known to us through the Acts of the Apostles.[1]

The scribes often gathered around them in the schoolroom a large number of pupils, whom they instructed thoroughly, free of charge. (This regulation was, however, evaded.)[2] Here it was that the new generation of learning was reared. The ideal was to engrave in the pupils' memory the exact words of the Master. To our way of thinking the instruction, with its eternal repetition, was mechanical, and ill designed to develop individual character. The influence of the scribes, again, extended far beyond the walls of the schoolroom. As experts in the current law they had in their hands, as a rule, the decision of actual

[1] Acts 22^{3}; cf. 5^{34-39}.

[2] Jesus even reproaches them with greed of gain; e.g., Mark 12^{40}, Matt. 23^{25}.

cases in the workaday world ;[1] they had a leading voice in the Synagogue. Wherever, in fact, advice was needed in questions which must be decided by means of the Old Testament their assistance was sought. They were treated everywhere with the utmost deference, and addressed as Rabbi, ' my master,' which subsequently became an actual title. Many resigned themselves very readily to such marks of esteem, or even demanded them. Beyond all doubt the picture which Jesus gives is painted from the life : ' They love the first couch at banquets and the first seat in the synagogue and the salutations in public squares, and to be addressed by people as " my master." '[2] In fact, then, the remark of Jesus is not too strongly phrased, ' the scribes and the Pharisees have set themselves on the chair of Moses.'[3]

Jesus here makes mention, beside the scribes, of another special group, that of the Pharisees. Over and over again in the gospels we find the scribes and Pharisees together. And the connexion between the two is of the closest, even though they do not coincide. ' Scribe ' is the more

[1] Even in the highest Jewish Court, the Sanhedrin, they had a preponderating influence.

[2] Matt. 23⁶ sq. [3] Matt. 23².

inclusive term. There certainly were scribes who belonged to another group whose acquaintance we shall make, that of the Sadducees. The Pharisees are the people who desire, in daily life, to follow exactly the directions of the scribes, the specifically 'religious' folk, the 'godly' of that age: but—in sharp contrast to the godly of past times, who had been oppressed by the rich and by evildoers—now the ruling class. Their chief task was to carry out, in the strictest and most scrupulous manner, the requirements of the Law together with the whole oral tradition, in the form which the labour of the scribes had given it. These 'godly' were regarded by the people as something set apart, as patterns of godliness: a fact which is proved by the name 'Pharisees,' which was probably attached to them by opponents. It means the 'separated,' that is, those who are distinguished from the bulk of the people by being peculiarly pure and godly. They called themselves *Haberim*, 'comrades,' and this name shows that they did not recognize every Jew as a comrade;[1] the answer they gave to the question, 'Who is my neighbour?'[2] was this: 'The group

[1] As the Old Testament enjoins. [2] Luke 10[29].

of those who realize most strictly the ideal of legal purity and piety.' (According to Josephus this group numbered six thousand.) They were conscious of being the élite of the people. It is self-evident that this must often have led to hypocritical arrogance. The extremely sharp polemic of Jesus against the Pharisees[1] has indeed had such an effect that, to the popular mind, a Pharisee and a hypocrite are one and the same thing. But we must be on our guard against a mistaken generalization. It is certain that the piety of many Pharisees was of a thoroughly earnest kind; they spared themselves not at all. Any other verdict would do grievous injustice not only to men like Hillel and Gamaliel, but also to innumerable others. But this only brings out more clearly the fact that those types which forced themselves to the front in public life, carried piety to market and demanded the admiration of the crowd, were justly scourged by Jesus as hypocrites. There is also no reason to doubt that at the time of Jesus' ministry the morbid and repulsive forms of Pharisaic godliness were so preponderant that, in a general review, no others needed to be

[1] Cf. especially Matt. 23.

considered. At the same time the piercing eye of Jesus could perceive and duly estimate the danger of arrogance and vainglory to which this ideal of piety must under all circumstances be exposed. In other matters, besides their conspicuous legalism, the Pharisees stood as representatives of orthodox belief; this might indeed be deduced from their essential character; they shared all the conceptions of their time with regard to angels and spirits, and believed in the resurrection of the dead.[1] The very questionable account of them in Josephus[2] gives no sure ground for deciding what they thought concerning the divine providence and human free will. In any case the Pharisees were not a special religious school in Judaism, though they have often been so represented, but simply a party which stood for the ideal of the legalistic Jews, as the course of development had shaped it—the ideal, in fact, for which every Jew ought to stand. It is also a mistake to regard the Pharisees as a political party. Their history, it is true, often shows

[1] Acts 23⁸.

[2] Josephus tries, in accordance with the taste of his readers, to depict the Pharisees, Sadducees, Essenes, and Zealots as philosophical schools.

them involved in political affairs. The earliest beginnings known to us of what afterwards became the Pharisaic group, namely the so-called Assidæans ('the pious') of the Maccabean time, stood in close connexion with the fighters for freedom, but only because the existence of legalistic piety was at stake. After the foundation, however, of a Maccabean dynasty, which had the conduct of politics in its own hands, the Assidæans severed the connexion, and a bitter opposition arose between the two, as we learn especially from the Psalms of Solomon. This began under Hyrcanus, and reached its climax under Alexander Jannæus. But the Pharisees were able to endure the government of Herod, and even the Roman overlordship. They had no necessary concern with politics. They would tolerate any kind of rule, so long as no hindrance was offered to the exercise of their godliness. A group, however, which was in a certain sense an offshoot from them,[1] pursued purely political ends; these were the Zealots,[2] who sought, weapon in hand, to bring about by force the great

[1] The Pharisee Zadduk was one of its founders.
[2] The 'men of violence,' Matt. 11[12], are Zealots.

change, the opening of a new era, the coming of the kingdom of God. But these revolutionaries, who set up the false Messiahs that led to the catastrophe of 70 A.D., must by no means be looked on as analogous to the Pharisees. Their development led, from the starting-point, in a quite different direction.

The Pharisees stood in contrast on the one hand to the common people and on the other hand to the Sadducees. The folk from whom the Comrades distinguished themselves were the *'Am-ha-ares*, the 'people of the land.' The Pharisee looked with disdain on the indifferent, uncultivated throng, which did not even know the Law and the Tradition, not to say observe them both punctiliously. It was the 'accursed multitude.'[1] Thus the expression 'Am-ha-ares,' which is used in the Old Testament, without any dishonourable association, of the people as distinct from the government, became a term of abuse, which was afterwards applied even to individuals—'he is an 'Am-ha-ares.' This rabble, then, included all the uncultured and indifferent, but especially the notorious sinners and the hated 'publicans,' who had debased

[1] John 7^{49}.

themselves to become tools of the foreign government in the collection of taxes. This explains the huge offence which the Pharisees took at the association of Jesus with the dregs of the people. Such disdain was to be found, at first, only on the side of the Pharisees. The lower strata of the people seem nevertheless to have looked up with a sort of timid admiration to the guardians of the Law and of godliness. But little by little a sense of irritation and hostility grew up, naturally enough, on the other side. The evidence for this, however, belongs to a later time.

The Pharisees were not only contrasted with those below them but also with those above them, for they stood in opposition to the Sadducees, who represented the priestly nobility. These were members of the leading sacerdotal families, and their name of Sadducees, 'those belonging to Sadduk,' was most probably intended to imply descent from the old priestly family of Zadok.[1] They were probably not united into a special group until the formation of the Pharisaic party gave occasion for such a union. Not that that party was in itself antagonistic to the priests;

[1] Cf. I Kings 2^{35}.

on the contrary, it performed all legal duties towards them with the utmost fidelity. Still it is easily intelligible that, in view of the growing influence of the scribes and Pharisees, the old noble families, from which the higher priests were drawn, felt compelled to take up a hostile attitude, since they saw their own leading position in danger. Since the Exile the high-priest had been at the same time the ruler of the people, and the foremost of his colleagues had been the diplomatic body, who conducted political affairs. It was highly important for them to keep the people under their influence, and any diminution of it threatened their position. Hence arose their opposition to the Pharisees, which again shaped the course of the priests themselves; for it is this which explains the fact that they recognized only the written Law, and rejected the whole tradition of which the Pharisees were champions. For the same reason they did not accept the new orthodoxy, especially the resurrection of the dead, nor yet the belief in angels and demons. As regards religion, then, they certainly stood at the time of Jesus behind their age, and below the level of the popular faith; in other matters, however, they were more far-sighted, and, it must be confessed, more worldly. They tried to live in peace with the Roman dominion, and had no reason for desiring a change. They were also the party most accessible to contemporary culture, though not in the same degree as formerly in the Græco-Syrian time, when they had even looked with complacency on the attempts of such a man as Antiochus Epiphanes. That was no longer possible, since in Jesus' time the Pharisees had already gained such a grasp of the reins that the Sadducees must always take them into account, if they wished to be any longer tolerated by the people. The power which they still possessed lay simply in the prestige of the Temple worship, which the Law enjoined, and in political affairs, which no one else understood. When both of these came to an end in 70 A.D. the Sadducees disappeared also, without leaving a trace, while the scribes remained, and enjoyed an undivided supremacy.

We have now only one more group to consider, a group which stands insulated like a foreign body in the midst of Judaism, the only one which breaks the uniformity of the Church, namely, the *Essenes*. The name probably means 'the pious.'

Fifteen years ago it was possible to doubt the existence of this group, or at least to despair of gaining any certain knowledge about them. The credibility of the most important authorities, Philo and Josephus, was at that time grievously shaken; but to-day they may be regarded as substantially reinstated. We must, however, in Philo's case, allow for the way in which he tries to exhibit the Essenes as approaching his own philosophy and method, and in that of Josephus for the somewhat strong Greek colouring which, in deference to his Græco-Roman public, he throws over them. A critical examination of these sources leads us to characterize the Essenes as a monastic order, a fellowship with a special type of worship, a mystic society. On Jewish soil they are the only example of *monasticism*, such as is to be found in other religions, for instance the Egyptian, Buddhist, and Christian. There were about four thousand of them in the towns and villages of Palestine, men only, living in special houses, in order to separate themselves from their compatriots and devote themselves to a pure and holy life. The novice must serve a probation of three years before being admitted, by a strict vow, into the order, in which all the members were bound together, under the rule of superiors, by community of goods—all private possessions were given up; money, food, and clothing were held in common—and by a definite regulation of the daily life. Field work and handiwork were framed about with prayer, ablutions, and refections. Their leading conceptions were simplicity, temperance, and, above all, purity; they wore a white habit, bathed often, avoided all pollution with the utmost care, and rejected marriage—probably to escape the defilement incident to association with the other sex. In certain ways the Essenes present the aspect of a separate community of worshippers; they took no part in the Jewish sacrificial worship, and rejected sacrifice altogether; baths and repasts played a great part in their life: both were sacred acts. Before every meal eaten in common a cold bath must be taken. Novices were not admitted to the bath for the first year. The purpose of these baths has nothing to do with the ordinary cleansing power of water, but with a mysterious, sacramental consecration of the whole man through its means. This explains how in cases where no external uncleanliness came into question, as when a full member of the order happened to touch a novice, the cold bath was enjoined. In the same way the common repast, prepared by the priest of the order, and partaken of in festal attire, was an act of worship. No stranger might take part in it. It was opened and closed with prayer. Solemn stillness reigned, as at some mystery. These acts of worship all point in the direction of a mystic society; and finally we must mention the secret writings and secret doctrine, which belong to the essence of a mystic society, and were also found among the Essenes. It is a very vexed question how this remarkable product of the Jewish religion came into being. All that is certain at present is that, though the fundamental character of the Essenes was Jewish, there are unmistakable traces of the influence of foreign religions. The Jewish element is seen in their monotheism, their reverence for the Mosaic Law, their strict observance of the Sabbath. Even their punctilious concern for purity connects them closely with the Pharisaic party. On the other hand their rejection of marriage, anointing, and sacrifice is not Jewish, nor yet their doctrine of the immortality of the soul; least of all their invocation of the sun. It cannot be doubted that what they beheld in the sun was the divine splendour, and this idea underlies their anxious precautions not to offend it by lack of reverence. It is questionable whether their repudiation of slavery and of the oath can conceivably be Jewish. We are not yet able to say with certainty whence the foreign elements to be observed among the Essenes were derived. Some investigators speak of contact with Greek (particularly neo-Pythagoræan and Orphic) religion, others of the influence of oriental religions, especially the Persian, Babylonian, and Mandæan. This second theory has already secured a preponderance of authority. The possibility of such a phenomenon as that of the Essenes in Palestine is one of the strongest proofs of the influence of foreign religions, and the degree in which it was exerted even in the mother-land of Judaism. This must be kept in mind when we consider certain points which we have not yet touched.

Now that we have finished our survey of the differences which existed in Judaism, we come back to the unity with which we started. The question at once arises along what paths the doctrine and piety of this Jewish Church took its course. The exposition given in the following chapter deals chiefly with the point of view of the scribes and Pharisees, but only because theirs was the chief pervasive and directive force within the church.

CHAPTER II

DOCTRINE AND PIETY IN THE CHURCH

THE two poles of all religion are God and man. We will ask first of all what was the nature of the Jewish belief in God, as it had taken shape in the thought and piety of the Church at the time of Jesus. The most striking fact is that God had been set, as it were, at a remote distance, and severed from man, and from the world at large, by a deep chasm. He sits enthroned, unapproachable, in the heavens. At the thought of God the pious soul is filled with holy awe. The continual effacement of those ingloriously human lineaments in God which were to be read of in the Old Testament can be understood and defended as a merit, implicit in a more spiritual conception; but the real far-removedness of God is seen in the fact that God's proper name, Jahweh, was used less and less in the post-exilic age, and at last might not be uttered at all. It became a secret name; it was only used in the Temple worship. Instead of it general expressions such as the Holy, the Almighty, the Sublime, the Great, the Lord of Heaven, the Lord of Lords, the King of Kings, the Glory, the Great Majesty, were used, and also the simple word 'Heaven.' This is the meaning of the word in Jesus' parable of the Prodigal Son: 'Father, I have sinned against heaven (that is, against God) and before thee.'[1] The 'Kingdom of God' and the 'Kingdom of Heaven' in the Gospels are therefore the same thing. This extrusion of the old name of Jahweh, the pronunciation of which was then forgotten, was by no means an insignificant matter. With the personal name the personal nearness of God is lost. God grows paler, fainter, more remote. Belief in a present Deity, glad faith in a God that manifests himself in actual experience, is much more rarely to be found. Occasionally, in times of national exaltation, it shines forth with its ancient power, as for example during the Maccabean war of liberty,[2]

[1] Luke 15[18] and [21]. [2] Cf. I Macc.

but these are exceptional moments.[1] As a rule God stands far aloof from the present time. No doubt this is closely connected with the fact that the present time was nearly always so sad and gloomy that none could summon up courage to hold such a faith. Indeed, even the old faith in the past, faith in the 'God of the fathers'—a favourite term—who had manifested himself in the choosing and historical guidance of the Jewish people, in the Covenant of Sinai and the giving of the Law, in the worship and the promises,[2] is rather an accepted heritage, piously transmitted, than a living good, fruitful for the life of to-day. The roots of the belief in God are now planted altogether in the future. Its fundamental note is, God will reveal himself out of the heavens, God will save, will raise from the dead, will judge the world. The time till then is, as Paul phrases it, a time which God overlooks, a time of divine long-suffering. And so, instead of a powerful confidence in the felt nearness of God, speculation spreads her wings, to speed with the help of

[1] The Psalms of Solomon may also be named in this connexion.

[2] Rom. 9^4.

phantasy into the far distance; not only the distant future, but also the beginnings of time; since the belief in a divine Creator, which expresses itself in glowing colours, by means sometimes of grotesque and fantastic images, is characteristic of late Judaism.[1] The reality of the cleft between God and man is shown by the different attempts which were made to bridge it over. In the first place the angels must be mentioned; they came between God and man, not side by side with God. Monotheism remains unimpaired;[2] but God is himself so remote, so unapproachable, that he has intercourse with the world through other beings. In this way the angels gain an independent importance. The very ancient belief in angels, which the prophets had forced into the background, revived more and more during the post-exilic period, and stands in its fullest vigour and elaboration at the time of Jesus.

Some of their names are known, such as Michael, Gabriel, Uriel, Raphael. They are arranged in classes, such as the four, six, or seven archangels

[1] Especially of the Ethiopic Enoch, the Slavonic Enoch, and Philo under the influence of non-Jewish ideas.

[2] This received expression in names like the Living, the Eternal, the Lord of spirits.

(to which the four here named belong), the cherubim and seraphim, and those dominions, principalities and powers which we meet in the New Testament.[1] Their occupations are known; and here simple old popular conceptions come again to life. Originally the stars were regarded as angels, and this is the meaning of the phrase 'the host of heaven.' This conception endured, or was only slightly modified, in the sense that the angels are in charge of the stars; they are the heavenly watchers. And like heaven, the earth too has its angels, yes, every part of it, wind and waves, thunder and lightning, beasts and plants. In this doctrine the oldest popular belief, according to which everything is filled with mysterious life, every tree and every fountain, celebrates its resurrection. And just as individual men have their guardian angels,[2] so in a special degree have the nations. Persia and Greece have their angels as well as the Jewish people. It is natural that belief should cling with peculiar fondness to the angel of the Jews. His name is Michael. He is the celestial secretary, who represents the nation, fights for the Jews, stands with them in the last

[1] E.g., Rom. 8^38; Eph. 1^21; Col. 1^16. [2] Matt. 18^10.

judgment. Finally, the nature of the angels is also known. They are celestial, spiritual beings, created by God, similar to man, but not subject to human needs. Besides the good angels there are also bad ones, about which we shall speak later. The most important point is that the religious longing to perceive the divine power in daily life is satisfied by means of the angels. They stand between man and God, who retires into the distance.

A like part is played by certain strange, hybrid forms, about which it is hard to say whether they are personal beings or abstractions. They were especially in favour in Alexandrian circles, but were also well known in the Judaism of Palestine. The Wisdom, Word, Glory or Shechina and Spirit of God are intermediate beings of this kind. As early as in the Proverbs we read about Wisdom, 'Jahweh created me as the beginning of his ways, as the first of his works of old. I have been installed from everlasting. . . . Then I was at his side as a master-workman, day by day I was pure delight, sporting busily at all times before him, sporting upon his earth, and had my delight among the sons of men.'[1] Is this only a poetic,

[1] Prov. 8^{22-31}.

artistic fancy, or does the writer intend to depict a personal being? In any case the further development, which we can trace in Jesus Sirach, the Wisdom of Solomon, and Philo, speaks definitely in favour of the latter. A similar significance attached—in Palestine, however, only at a later period—to the Word of God, especially the creative Word, conceived in the light of Genesis i. An iridescent indefiniteness was still characteristic of these figures. In a number of cases we cannot decide whether they are to be taken for mere attributes and activities of God or for independent beings. But there is an unmistakable tendency towards independent life. That peculiar ambiguity has its intrinsic justification in the fact that the purpose of these beings is twofold, on the one hand to establish a communication with God, on the other hand to prevent a direct connexion between God and the World. Accordingly they appear sometimes as aspects of the divine being, sometimes as independent. From time to time in Jewish literature the Law, that centre of the doctrine of piety in the Church, and indeed of Jewish life in general, is treated almost in the same way as an independent, spiritual entity. It is the embodied

Will of God, his embodied Wisdom, and here too it so falls out that this great something, which is the ruler of life, has a substantiality of its own. God himself retires behind it. It is specially recorded that at the giving of the Law, alongside other marvels, angelic powers took part.[1] Supernatural glory surrounds the form of Moses, the lawgiver. A whole legendary cycle has been spun about this greatest of men, who up to the time of Jesus was looked on also as a prophet, and, as in the case of Elijah, it ends with an ascension into heaven.[2] Whether we turn to Jesus Sirach, Philo, or Josephus, all are at one in the glorification of the Law. This leads us immediately to the attitude adopted by the Jew towards God.

God, as lord and king, has given his people the Thora, the Law. Accordingly the highest task of the Jew consists in submission and obedience to this Law. And since for the oriental mind the king is a despot, and his subjects are his servants, so also the Jew has not only to obey the Law where he understands it, but, like a menial,

[1] Acts 7^{35}; Heb. 2^{2}; Gal. 3^{19}.

[2] The significance of these ascensions (cf. also that of Enoch) should be considered from the point of view of historical religion in connexion with the ascension of Jesus.

blindly and at all points. This explains his tenacious observance of the ceremonial prescriptions. Nobody could discover for what reason certain foods and drinks must be forbidden, why a dead person makes you ceremonially unclean, and a bath makes you ceremonially clean again. Even Jewish scribes have openly confessed so much. In all such questions there was but one answer: it is the will of the heavenly king, whom we must obey. The genuinely oriental character of Jewish devotion showed itself in the quite especial zeal with which these ceremonial regulations were observed. In this respect the Diaspora does not lag behind the Judaism of Palestine. It was precisely in ceremonies, primarily in circumcision, in the strict observance of the Sabbath, in the numerous rules of diet and so forth, that the peculiarity of the Jew was to be found, which severed him so strikingly from the Gentile nations, and forced itself on their notice as a mark of difference. These rules, again, were pre-eminently the object of the labour of the scribes. It was one of their chief tasks to preserve faithfully all special injunctions, to build up general rules, to catch and bind the whole multiform, mobile life of the people in a network of such directions. This it is which, more than anything else, stamps upon later Judaism the character of narrowness, paltriness, and often of ridiculous futility. It had not always been so. Even in the proverbial wisdom of the Jews there still lived a consciousness that the Law has a greater boon to bestow, that its aim is to point the way to true morality. Certainly the ceremonial law had never been disregarded. The historical situation in the post-exilic period was what gave it its great importance; it was a necessity, to ensure the existence of the community. The actual narrowing, the one-sided emphasis laid upon this side, was the result of the activity of the scribes. This was in the mind of Jesus when he said about them and about the Pharisees, 'They bind heavy burdens and lay them on men's shoulders, but they themselves will not move them with their finger.'[1] Under this yoke sighed the weary and heavy-laden, whom Jesus called to himself.[2] And yet they submit. It is the will of God, which must be obeyed: what more can be said? It is well known with what tenacity and passionate energy

[1] Matt. 23⁴. [2] Matt. 11²⁸⁻³⁰.

the Jews pressed on to this goal, even to the laying down of their lives; how in time of war they let themselves be massacred rather than resist on the Sabbath; with what unbending antagonism they opposed the attempts of Antiochus Epiphanes to introduce Greek customs by force; and how in times of peace, especially under the Roman emperors, they struggled again and again to obtain such privileges as would allow them to live according to the Law.

It was of especial and, beyond question, of fateful importance that the Mosaic Law was at the same time, in Palestine, the civil law.[1] All relations and conditions of public and private life were regulated in accordance with the Mosaic Law and the exposition of the Scribes. These formed the basis of decisions in the local courts, such as the Sanhedrin, the supreme court of justice in Jerusalem. The execution of capital punishment alone was reserved by the Romans.[2] Even the most impossible laws to be kept in

[1] In the Diaspora matters were essentially different. As a rule, so far as they had no privileges, the Jews were obliged to conform to the law of the land.

[2] Still, a Gentile who forced his way into the inner court of the Temple was liable to the death penalty without conditions.

operation, such as the remission of debts every seventh year, which would have destroyed all credit, remained in force, though they were deprived of their real meaning by the additions of the Scribes. But this close connexion between religious and civil law reacted fatally upon piety; piety towards God was looked upon, in the main, as something juristic. In Judaism religion and law entered into a close alliance, to the grievous hurt of religion. The peculiar character of legal piety had already brought it about that attention was directed and importance attached, more and more, to the single individual. In the pre-exilic period the individual could take shelter under the people, since God had made his covenant immediately with the people as a whole, but as the power of the Law grew individualism made its way also. For every man the question was whether he himself fulfilled the Law or not. The unity of the people is cleft in two; on one side of the gulf stand the pious, on the other the godless—the great mass of the indifferent and lukewarm stand over against the élite of the serious. Indeed, it does not help the individual to belong to the group of the pious; every one must be answerable for his own deeds. But this development of the idea of piety, which in itself is really progressive, was vitiated by the circumstance that the relation of the single soul to God was regarded almost exclusively from a legal standpoint. God was looked upon, therefore, chiefly as a judge. It is true that the individual Jew in the time of Jesus speaks of God also as his father. In applying the name of father to God Jesus did nothing new. But, apart from the fact that use of this name in Jewish literature is not very frequent,[1] the glad, confident, childlike feeling which the name of father on the lips of Jesus implied is nowhere to be found. God is not thought of chiefly as father, but as judge. His great attribute is justice, understood now in the juristic sense. At one time justice, or righteousness, was the judgment of God sounding forth salvation, attesting his faithfulness towards himself and the people with which he had made a covenant. This meaning is prominent in the second Isaiah and in the Psalms. Justice and grace stood in the most intimate relation with one another. Now justice means the activity of the judge in

[1] The Wisdom of Solomon forms an exception.

requiting or compensating according to the letter of the Law. The pious receive their reward, the impious their punishment.[1] True, mention is still often, indeed very often, made of the grace and mercy which the Almighty shows towards his feeble creatures; the Wisdom literature seeks to combine grace and justice by the thought of the education of the individual; but, taken as a whole, grace now stands as a second thing, alongside justice, in a wavering, uncertain posture. The consequence for the pious man is that everything depends on his ability to stand uncondemned in the just judgment of God, and if possible to gain his grace. Righteousness before God, justification—these are the concepts—in which Paul, that pupil of the Pharisees, frames his thought. But since God's will is only to be learned from his Law, it is now easy to understand the eager, sedulous solicitude of the Jew to observe this Law with scrupulous strictness; and not only the Law itself, but also the whole appendix of tradition which professed to be derived from it. If possible he would do more than the Law commands. By supererogatory good deeds

[1] Cf. Rom. 2[6].

it is possible to win merit in the eyes of God. These views have been taken over directly by the Catholic Church. Piety is cankered through and through by the thought of reward. In the future judgment God has nothing to do but to give the Jew his due according to the letter of the Law, according to the preponderance of good deeds or bad, or any merit which he happens to have in hand. How extraordinarily deep-rooted this thought was in the time of Jesus is best seen in the fact that Jesus himself, whose inner feeling had completely escaped from such a scheme, often startles us by expressing his ideas in terms of reward and punishment.

These ideas as a whole had necessarily a twofold effect on the mood of those who held them; it oscillated between fear and presumption. The pious man has before his eyes the coming judgment day of God, when the dead shall arise and receive their sentence. Has he trod the way of life or of death?[1] Will he hold his own amid all the need, anxiety, and seduction of this present age? At the end of his life will his account show a

[1] For the doctrine of the two ways, cf. e.g., 'Testament of the Twelve Patriarchs,' Asher, 1; Matt. 7^{13} sq.

balance on the credit side, a surplus of good deeds over bad ? Will he find grace before the severe judge ? Trembling and misgiving must seize the Jew, the best Jews most of all, at these thoughts ; such misgiving as speaks in the words of IV Ezra : 'All that are born are deformed with impieties, full of sins, laden with guilt. It were much better for us, if after death we had not to enter into the judgment.'[1] Paul as a Pharisee, before his conversion to Christianity, must have tested all these feelings, as we learn from the Epistle to the Romans.[2] It is this quivering dread which engendered the penitential sense that is so markedly characteristic of later Judaism. It found expression in penitential ceremonies, prayers and psalms. The Jews are driven to penance by the consciousness of sin, and also, it must be granted, by sorrow under the sufferings which were still to some extent regarded, according to ancient Israelite belief, as a divine punishment. Penance consists above all things in contrition, repentance, confession, and is combined with

[1] IV Ezra 7^{68} sq.

[2] The celebrated description in Rom. 7^{7-23} was written by the apostle in retrospect on his Jewish past, in contrast to his present life as a Christian.

self-chastisement (fasting, mourning 'in sack-cloth and ashes'). Penance is supposed to make atonement.[1] At the time of Jesus' ministry this state of mind must have been widely diffused. John the Baptist had sounded the call to repentance, with extraordinary success. Jesus had taken it up and made it the basis of his whole preaching; this note is heard throughout; but it is momentously transformed, and recalls the demands of the prophets.[2] Jesus turned his eyes from the externals of penance, and by repentance meant a change of spirit. But he found the conception, as well as the feeling, in the Judaism of his day. The terrors of the year 70 A.D. mightily strengthened the penitential feeling, so that it continues to play a leading part in the later Jewish theology. And the same misgiving which drove men to penance also urged the pious man into busy efforts to serve God by works. To do as much as possible, to exceed, if he could, the necessary measure—who knows, it might not be enough, after all! This is, however, only one side of the matter. By the side of dread stands

[1] Cf. the Testament of the Twelve Patriarchs, Asher, I.

[2] E.g., Ezekiel 18^{31}; Hosea 10^{12}; Jeremiah 4^{3}.

presumption. Outwardly, indeed, it is more prominent, since it was in churchly circles, among the pious, that it chiefly prevailed. The masses of the people, who sighed under the burden of the demands of the Law and the tradition of the fathers, men whose social circumstances left them neither time nor opportunity for the sedulous observance of such rules, can hardly have been inclined, as a rule, to such overweening assurance. But the pious, the Pharisees, who really put themselves to the greatest trouble and could never do enough to satisfy themselves, often looked on their own performances with complacency, and disparaged others. The Gospels afford an inexhaustible supply of instances. The form of the Pharisee who prays, 'God, I thank thee that I am not as the rest of men . . . I fast twice in the week; I give tithes of all that I possess,'[1] is copied, in its vain self-glorification and arrogance direct from real life. With what contempt did the words about Jesus fall from such lips, 'the associate of publicans and sinners.'[2] This type of the pious Pharisee is incomparably depicted by Paul, when he says that he relies upon the Law,

[1] Luke 18^{11} sq. [2] Matt. 11^{19}.

glories in God and knows his will, tests the differences (between good and bad), being instructed by the Law, and is confident that he is a guide of the blind, a light to those that are in darkness, an instructor of the foolish, a teacher of infants.[1] That same laborious zeal in the service of works which is born of dread of the judge serves on the other hand as a foundation for self-confidence and presumption. The superficiality which measures itself by those whom it regards as worse engenders admiration of its own proficiency. The consciousness of piety poisons piety to the very marrow.

While we have realized the destructive effect of the alliance between religion and law upon piety, we must not forget that morality was also grievously damaged. The one fact that the standard in moral matters as in all else was the written Law was, in itself, a source of grave detriment. In the Law the preponderant element was prohibition. Thus with regard to morality, as well as the rest, what was above all things laid down was what a man ought not to do. There is, in fact, no more significant acknowledgment of this state of things

[1] Rom. 2^{17-20}.

than the formula delivered to us repeatedly by Jewish lips, 'What thou wilt not that men do unto thee, do thou not unto another.'[1] It must be granted that this is the whole width of heaven apart from that word of Jesus which kindles the energy of moral action, 'Whatsoever ye would that men should do to you, do ye unto them.'[2] There was not, then, very much in the Law which could be applied in the manifold relations of life. The whole work of developing and refining the general principles, and to a certain extent that of giving them currency for use in daily life, was relegated to the individual, and so stood outside the Law, as a thing left to freedom, or rather to caprice. The Law contained so many specific demands that all cases not mentioned might appear to be abandoned to the opinion of the individual. This explains why the Jewish proverbial wisdom treats the whole field of private morality from the standpoint of the sane, intelligent, worldly wisdom of a cultured man, who enquires about practical utility. Alongside the ecclesiastical, legal ethic there grew up, then, a utilitarian morality of independent importance,

[1] E.g., by Hillel and Philo. [2] Matt. 7[12].

which coheres but loosely with religion. Finally, a morality so closely connected with the Law was only considered binding between Jews and Jews, just as the Law had been given the Jews as their peculiar distinction. A few ethical directions in the Law itself refer definitely to strangers; apart from these everything was regarded as applying to Jews alone. The morality is narrow and exclusive. Even in the writings of a man of such high culture and breadth of view as Jesus Sirach we read, 'Arouse thine anger (O God) and shake forth thy wrath, root out the adversary and grind the enemy. . . . Break into pieces the heads of the princes of thine enemies, that say: there is none beside us.'[1] These are words which remind us of the worst imprecatory Psalms. There were also, of course, milder and more broad-minded characters; we need but think of Hillel and Philo. The missionary impulse, the propaganda, led to mitigations. But on the whole we find, even in the moral dealings of the Jews, that exclusion of all but themselves which, on the other hand, drew the bitter hatred of all foreigners upon their race. The way in which this exclusive

[1] 33^{8-12}.

feeling had a certain effect even on Jesus is clearly seen in the fact that he felt himself sent, in the first place, only to his own people, and forbade the mission to the Gentiles and Samaritans.[1] In post-exilic times this feeling underwent a very distressing development; it was applied in practice even to members of the Jewish race. When various groups stood sharply contrasted and severed from one another, above all the groups of the pious and the ungodly, the members of one circle thought themselves at liberty to treat those of another as Gentiles, or even worse. Here again a well-meaning man like Jesus Sirach may serve as a typical example. 'Give to the pious and take not the part of the sinner, do good to the meek and give not to the ungodly . . . for even the Highest hateth the sinner, and requiteth the ungodly with chastisement.' The pious man conceived his God in his own image, and he hated the ungodly, even among his own compatriots, as he hated a Gentile. Morality bears the character of sectarian arrogance. Jesus has raised an eternal monument to this type of feeling in the well-known parable of the Good Samaritan.[2] In

[1] Matt. 15[24]; 10[5] sq., if spoken by Jesus. [2] Luke 10[30-37].

the course of the first Christian century the bitter antagonism between Pharisees and *'Am-ha-ares* passed all bounds.

These were the chief ways in which morality was prejudiced by its mere connexion with the Law; there were others which resulted from the juristic character of the Law. What a judge has to enforce is the wording of the statute. In the same way all moral demands seemed to be fulfilled when the letter of the Law was obeyed. This is what gives Paul occasion to call Judaism the covenant of the letter, and to declare that the letter killeth.[1] And its influence upon the very breath of life of all true morality, such as springs forth from a right state of the spirit, is indeed mortal. A flaming denunciation of the chaining together of the letter and morality is given us in the first great section of the Sermon on the Mount, in which Jesus brings out again and again just the one truth, that an ethical demand is very far from being satisfied by observance of its mere wording; rather, as the whole Sermon shows, the whole weight must be laid on the spiritual state in which the single act takes its rise. Closely

[1] II Cor. 3^6.

connected with the moral literalism of the Jews is this further fact, that everything which oversteps the letter of the Law—praiseworthy as it is from the point of view of ordinary good sense and practical wisdom—gains the character of something supererogatory, something to be rewarded. Another result of the amalgamation of Law and righteousness was not less dangerous. Amid the mass of particular injunctions the moral commands lost their unique dignity, lost their place of eminence above the ceremonial regulations. They were so little, amid so much. And often enough, through human indolence and the base instincts of our race, that little was allowed to be hid behind the big bulk of the rest. The moral commands were much more difficult to obey, because they required a much higher degree of self-conquest. This was what Jesus had in mind when he said to the Pharisees, 'Ye tithe all mint, dill, and cumin, and leave undone the hard part of the law, righteousness, mercy, and faithfulness.'[1] We know perfectly well that the judgment of these words did not fall on all Pharisees. There were noble figures among them, who had not lost the

[1] Matt. 23[23].

consciousness that the fulfilment of the Law is something which involves the whole conduct of life. But the danger which arose out of the juristic character of the Law was always there, and very many must have succumbed to it. In the closest possible connexion with this stood that hypocrisy with which Jesus, in such an extremely bitter style, reproaches the scribes and Pharisees. In the great discourse against the Pharisees, Matt. 23, from verse 13 onwards, there are seven Woes, which all except one[1] begin with the words, 'Woe to you, scribes and Pharisees, hypocrites!' Assuredly there cannot have been many who were consciously hypocritical, even though there were some who speculated with their exemplary piety on the admiration of the people.[2] What roused the indignation of Jesus to such a pitch was, fundamentally, the intrinsic untruth of the whole system. Behind the fair whitewash on the sepulchres he saw dead men's bones.[3] Piety which has severed itself from the spring of a really good spirit is, consciously or unconsciously, hypocrisy.

If we now turn to those exercises of worship in

[1] Matt. 23^{16}. [2] Matt. 6^{1-6}; 23^{5}. [3] Matt. 23^{27}.

which this piety was active, we find the Law penetrating into this field too. The whole Temple worship and everything connected with it is carried out with such punctilious fidelity because the Law commands it. That is the dominating point of view. At first sight it is indeed an astonishing and remarkable thing that the Pharisees, the violent opponents of the priestly Sadducæan nobility, fulfil all their ritual duties with a fidelity not to be surpassed, and even when possible outstrip the commandment of the Law—and in all this are only strengthening the back and filling the purse of their priestly opponents. The solution of this apparent contradiction lies in the fact that these ritual duties are enjoined in the Law, and therefore must be fulfilled.

In consequence of this the Temple with its priesthood and its worship enjoyed the highest respect and authority until its destruction in 70 A.D. The glory which had surrounded the sanctuary of Solomon in ancient days was not forgotten, and still had its effect. And the new sanctuary of Herod stood there in its splendour. 'See, what stones, what buildings!' exclaimed the disciples, in astonishment, to Jesus;[1] and so may many a pilgrim have cried, with admiration and awe, when he came with the throng of his fellows to Jerusalem for one of the great feasts. For those who dwelt in and around Jerusalem the Temple had a quite special importance. Every day crowds came in to the sacrifices, of which, in accordance with the penitential feeling of the time, the sin-offerings were valued most highly. The great Day of Atonement, with its expiation for the whole people and the whole land, was the chief festival. The laity were blessed by the priests, and delighted in the splendid ceremonial. The stay in Jerusalem—as we should now express it—was very interesting. There was always something to see—teachers with their pupils, disputations, private sacrifices, the arrival of strangers. And even the Jew who remained far off was filled with satisfaction and thankfulness that for him too, morning and evening, the burnt-sacrifices ascended to heaven. Against this, on the other hand, very considerable dues had to be met—the Temple tax, the gifts for sacrifices, which fell wholly or in part to the priests, the firstlings and first-fruits,

[1] Mark 13[1].

the tithe, payment of which was treated above all as a serious duty, personal presents, and so forth. And all this for the sake of the Law, as Jesus Sirach clearly says, 'Appear not before the face of the Lord with empty hands, for all these [sacrifices] are needful, since he has commanded them.'[1] The violent denunciation of sacrifices by the prophets had not indeed been forgotten. The same Sirach, who in 32^{1}, begins with the words, 'He that observes the Law offers many sacrifices,' says four verses later, 'The good pleasure of the Lord is gained by abstaining from sin, and his appeasement by abstaining from unrighteousness.' Still, for the letter's sake, the Sadducæan priesthood was not merely endured but highly honoured. In spite, however, of all this outward devotion religion had already severed itself, unconsciously, from the Temple cultus. Jesus had no occasion to attack it. Among the Essenes the separation was open and avowed. And thus the disappearance of the Temple was endured without any grave crisis ensuing.

The institution which really corresponded to the new individual piety was one which had arisen

[1] 32^{6} sq.

at the same time, one which was not commanded in the Law, the spiritual worship of the synagogue. But even in this second and most important outward manifestation of piety the Law was a decisive factor. We recognize this as soon as we realize what went on in the synagogue service.

Its external guidance lay in the hands of a president, the so-called archisynagogus ('ruler of the synagogue,' Luke 13^{14}), who was most probably chosen from the elders of the civil community. The service began with a confession, the so-called *Sh^ema'* ('hear!'), a compilation of passages from the Law. (There is a high degree of certainty that it existed in the time of Jesus.) Then followed a prayer, spoken standing, with face turned to Jerusalem. One member, called on by the president, spoke for all; the rest responded with an occasional Amen. The chief element, which came next, consisted in two lessons from the Hebrew text, accompanied by a Syrian translation. First a passage from the Law was read, the *Parasha*, 'section.' In this way the whole Law was gradually read aloud. Then came a passage from the prophets, the *Haphtara*, 'conclusion' (i.e., of the reading of scripture).

The lessons could be read, and the sermon which followed could be preached, by any of the members who were capable and willing. The service closed with a blessing, which was spoken if possible by a priest or Levite. Alms, too, in money or kind, were collected in the synagogue by special officials.

In this kind of public worship three points are especially prominent. We notice first its singularly democratic character. The powers of the officials, the president, the two or three alms-collectors, and the servant of the synagogue, were concerned only with external matters; the conduct of the service lay intrinsically in the hands of the congregation. Anyone might speak, avow his faith, pray, read, preach. Jesus himself, for instance, spoke in the synagogue. It was of course only natural that the high repute and technical knowledge of the scribes should gradually win for them, here as elsewhere, a predominant influence. In the second place, then, we remark the didactic character of the whole institution. In the centre of its procedure stands the scripture lesson, more especially the reading of the Law. Even the sermon was as a rule a practical comment on the law. The members of the congregation assemble to be instructed in the Law. Our Gospels speak of 'the teaching in the synagogue.' On the other hand the ceremonial elements are by no means prominent. What calls, however, for the highest praise is the entire absence of magical or sacramental features; the whole service lives and moves in a purely spiritual sphere. Its great resemblance to our Christian services, for which it has served as a direct model, is obvious to all. Among the people the synagogue services were highly esteemed; they were really popular. The sentence of exclusion from the synagogue, which was probably spoken by the elders of the congregation, was regarded as the severest of punishments.[1]

In connexion with the synagogue worship certain pious exercises were especially cultivated in everyday life—the study of the Law, prayer, almsgiving. It was the sign of a pious Israelite to be busied with the Law as much as possible, even outside the synagogue. As Hillel says, 'an ignorant man cannot be truly pious,' and 'the more knowledge of the Law, the more life.'[2] It

[1] Cf. Luke 6^{22}; John 9^{22}, 12^{42}, 16^{2}.
[2] Recorded in the Pirke Aboth.

was an ideal of life to repeat and ponder the Law in time of work and of recreation. This conception finds its classical expression in the late introduction to our collection of Psalms in the Old Testament: 'Well for the man who wanders not in the counsel of the wicked, nor walks the way of sinners, nor sits in the seat of those that mock, but delights in the Law of Yahweh, and meditates upon his Law day and night.'[1] Closely associated with the study of the Law was the practice of prayer, for which precise directions existed in the time of Jesus. The *Sh^{e}ma'*, which we have already referred to, was uttered morning and evening. Another prayer which certainly existed, at least in the main, was the *Sh^{e}moneh-esreh*, 'the prayer of eighteen supplications,' a really beautiful and pregnant petition—only somewhat too long—which was to be repeated, according to a later rule, morning, noon, and evening. Let us cite some of its loftiest thoughts as examples. 'Praised be thou, O Lord our God, and God of our fathers . . . Thou art almighty for ever, O Lord, that makest the dead to live . . . Thou art holy, and thy name is holy[2] . . . Praised be

[1] Psalm 1^1 sq. [2] A reminiscence of this in our Paternoster.

thou, O Lord, the giver of knowledge . . . Praised be thou, O Lord, that hast pleasure in a contrite heart. Forgive us, our father, for we have sinned.[1] . . . Praised be thou, O Lord, the redeemer of Israel. Hallow us, O Lord, and we shall be holy; help us, and we shall be holpen; for thou art our praise.' Prayers at table, thanksgivings before and after meat, were also in general use; Jesus himself used them. Then came private prayers. Beyond all doubt this tenderest blossom of the religious life was much injured by the coercion of rules, especially if we should suppose the much more detailed prescriptions of the Mishna to have been in force in Jesus' lifetime. But the necessity of repeating one and the same lengthy prayer several times a day, and the same prayer every day, must of itself lead in the end to a mere mechanical gabble. This fate has befallen the Paternoster, down to our own time, and no formulated church prayers can escape it. The prayerful ostentation of the Pharisees, who spoke prayers aloud as they walked the streets—their long petitions, with no heart in them—are known to us through the Gospels.[2]

[1] Reference to previous foot-note.

[2] Matt. 6[5], 15[8]; Mark 12[40].

And just as the alms were collected in the synagogue, in order to be distributed afterwards, so also the pious Jew used to give freely in other ways to the poor. Compassion and alms-giving were interchangeable terms. The literature is full of exhortations to beneficence, in which we can clearly see the special connexion between pious works and membership of the church. The best known passage comes from the Book of Tobit: 'Laudable is prayer with fasting and mercy and righteousness . . . For beneficence saves from death and cleanses from every sin.'[1] The value of alms can hardly be rated higher. It belongs to the range of things in which merit, and thereby propitiation, can be soonest attained. In the passage just quoted fasting is named in the closest connexion with prayer and alms. Although not commanded in the Law, except on the great Day of Atonement, yet as a consequence of the post-exilic penitential feeling the practice of fasting had become extraordinarily popular as a token of great piety. General fasts were held especially in times of severe need, for instance in times of drought, and

[1] 12⁸ sq.

always on Monday and Thursday. Of course no limit was set to private fasting. Among the Pharisees there were exemplary saints to be found who fasted every week on those two days, and were it is true, extremely conscious of the fact.[1] He who would be pious must fast, and was very willing that his fasting should not be concealed.[2] The disciples of John the Baptist used to fast, and Jesus and his disciples fell sadly under suspicion, because they did not fast.[3] This practice has simply been taken over by the Christian Church from the Jewish. Apart from ceremony and public worship the most notable manifestations of Church piety were almsgiving, prayer, and fasting. It is no accident that these three points form the subject of the second section of the Sermon on the Mount.[4]

[1] Luke 18^{12}. [2] Matt. 6^{16}. [3] Mark 2^{18}. [4] Matt. 6$^{1-18}$.

CHAPTER III

POPULAR PIETY

IT must be emphasized at the outset that no contrast is intended between the piety of the church and that of the people. What we have been reviewing was certainly, in the first place, the doctrine and piety of those circles which regarded themselves as especially pious, and exercised a determining influence in the Jewish Church, the circles of the Scribes and Pharisees. But the masses stood under that influence, and were attached to the church. They accepted as truth, which ought to be believed, that which was expounded to them in school and synagogue, and they conformed to the piety of the Pharisees. Still it was inevitable, then as now, that in the faith of the people there was much which bore a very different aspect from that of its original meaning. In the first place, it is important to note that the belief which the people held was only a fraction of that of the church. Much of what the leading church circles believe is unknown and unintelligible to the people ; much lies outside the possible range of popular belief or conception. For instance, the doctrine of those strange hybrids such as Wisdom, the Word, the Shechina, which we have examined, can hardly have been known among the people, and so far as it was known it can scarcely have been understood. On the other hand it was impossible for the people to observe the multitude of particular commands and traditions which the scribes put forward. They had neither time nor money enough for that. In fact, exemplary piety was only possible for those who were in tolerably good circumstances. There was always going on, therefore, in the popular religion a process of selection ; and, alongside that, a coarsening process, which is difficult to lay hold of in detail, but was undoubtedly at work. We may be sure, for instance, that the ideas concerning angels took, in the minds of the people, a much more realistic and concrete form—that downright belief in demons and devils about which we shall speak later. Such a coarsening process may easily result in an actual transformation of belief. It is exceedingly likely that in the popular faith the angels received a prominence which endangered monotheism itself. This affords the best explanation of that angel-worship which is assailed in the New Testament, for instance in the Epistle to the Colossians, the Epistle to the Hebrews, and the Revelation of John. Then again, popular piety always contains residuary, belated elements, which the more instructed have already surmounted. Views which were once general are held to with remarkable tenacity by the people. In the religion of the church a belief prevails in retribution in a world to come; but among the people the ancient belief in a retribution in *this* world is ineradicable—the belief which meets us in the Old Testament Psalms, the Psalms of Solomon, and in the New Testament, that the pious are prosperous on the earth, and that suffering is punishment.[1] The religious development had left that belief far behind. In the new church piety individualism, the decisive importance of the single personality, had asserted itself with power; but among the people the

[1] Cf. e.g., in the New Testament: Luke 13^{1-5}; John 9^{1-3}.

national idea was inveterately rooted, the feeling that the Jewish people, as such, was favoured by God. Among the masses it was still a distinctive and glorious title that they were 'the Israelites, to whom belong the sonship and the glory and the covenants and the giving of the Law and the service and the promises, to whom the fathers belong.'[1] God belongs to his own people, and that people to God. He cannot abandon it; he must needs save it. Nothing illustrates this national feeling more strikingly than the fact that in 70 A.D., just before the end, many of the Jews who were pent up in the besieged city believed firmly and fixedly, up to their last breath, that God would intervene, in view of the final catastrophe, and miraculously rescue them. This national element is the decisive trait in the piety of the people. At this point we must expressly point out that it offers no contrast to the feeling of the leading church circles. The Pharisees cherished the national hopes of Israel. They too believed in the Messiah. Every day, in the Sh^{e}moneh-esreh, the prayer was offered, 'May the scion of David thy servant soon spring forth, and

[1] Rom. 9[4] sq.

lift up his horn through thy help; for we wait upon thy help every day. Praised be thou, O Lord, that makest to spring forth a horn of salvation.' The Psalms of Solomon themselves, which most strongly reflect the popular expectation of a Messiah, are conceived from the standpoint of Pharisaic piety. But the difference of shade was, in this case, very significant. Among the church circles, among the Pharisees, the national expectancy was less prominent. What filled, for them, the whole range of present thought and action was the Law, and it afforded them a satisfaction which prevailed even under circumstances of great depression. But among the people all this was reversed. Even if we leave the Zealots, the national fanatics, quite on one side, the ordinary people, who felt the oppression of the political situation and the evil times most severely, lived in the national thought, and clung to it with all the warmth of their feeling, with all the force of their imagination, with all the wistfulness of hope. At the time when Jesus appeared the popular piety of the Jews was entirely concerned with the future. Out of the miserable present, in which the people dragged on a dreary existence under the iron rule of Rome, the most glowing hopes went forth towards what was soon to come. The great mass of the people lived outside the present, in a future which was awaited with feverish suspense. 'The kingdom of God and Messiah' was the watch-word of their religion. When Jesus appeared John the Baptist stood on the bank of Jordan and preached to great throngs that the kingdom of God and the Messiah were at hand.[1] It was a message to the people.[2] There are three points in which the national elements in this popular feeling can be discerned—in the way in which the kingdom of God and the kingdom of the Jews merge into one another, in their conception of the Messiah, in the fate of other nations.

It had long been an established idea among the Jews that Israel had but one king, Yahweh, beside whom no other had place. The Maccabean rising formed an exception, which, after the fall of the Hasmonean family, was quickly corrected. The Idumean dynasty of the Herods had always been hateful to the Jews, as a sacrilegious presumption. The kingship or the kingdom of Yahweh

[1] Matt. 3^{2} and ^{11} sq. [2] Matt. 3^{5-7}.

had been spoken of in the Old Testament in numerous places, in the Prophets, the Psalms and elsewhere, either in the sense that it was present and always existed,[1] or in the other sense that it was to come in the future.[2] Both ideas continued to appear in the later Jewish literature; but in the time of Jesus, and indeed much earlier, perhaps ever since Daniel, the *coming* of the kingdom had gained preponderance, and swayed the souls of the people in one direction. When John the Baptist and Jesus proclaimed the message, 'The kingdom of God is at hand,' when Jesus taught his disciples to pray, 'Thy kingdom come,' the deepest yearning of the people found expression. Every Jew understood thereby that the hidden rule of God should be plainly manifested, that his kingdom should appear visibly upon the earth: but their faith had a reverse side—in the minds of the Jews this kingdom was *their* kingdom. This fact nowhere appears more luminously than in Daniel 7^{27}, where the last time, after the judgment, is spoken of: 'Then shall the kingdom and the dominion and the greatness of the kingdoms under the whole heaven be given to

[1] Ex. 15^{18}; Ps. 145^{13}. [2] Is. 24^{23}; Micah 4^{7}.

the people of the saints of the Most High; his kingdom shall be an everlasting kingdom, and all dominions shall serve and be subject to him.' Here the place of the eternal kingdom of God is taken by the eternal kingdom of the people of the saints, that is to say, of the Jews. True, it is God who brings the coming kingdom, but it is in fact the Jewish kingdom. The national definiteness of Jewish expectation appears here very clearly. Accordingly the kingdom of the last time will be situated in Palestine; its centre will be Jerusalem and the Temple, both splendidly glorified. From all the ends of the earth the scattered Jews shall be summoned home by the great trumpets of God[1] (thus Jesus Sirach, Tobit, the Psalms of Solomon, etc.) and then a golden age shall begin in the new kingdom; fertility like that of Paradise, abundant progeny, child-birth without throes, no sorrow or sighing, but rest and peace. The deeper religious and moral conceptions of the vision of God, the consummation of sonship, purity and holiness are not absent, but are decidedly less prominent than these nationalist ideas. There are not many descrip-

[1] With a reminiscence of Is. 27^{13}.

tions of the future age which stand upon such a height as the concluding words of the Psalms of Solomon, 18^{6-9}: 'Blessed is he that shall live in these days and may behold the salvation of the Lord, which he is preparing for the generation to come under the rod of chastisement of the anointed of the Lord in the fear of his God, in spiritual wisdom, righteousness and strength, that he may lead everyone in works of righteousness through the fear of God, and present them all together before the face of the Lord, a good generation full of the fear of God in the days of grace.' These beautiful words bring us to the consideration of him that was to play a special part in the coming kingdom of God—the Messiah.

Ever since the time of the prophet Isaiah the Jewish people had been hoping for the Messiah, that is 'the anointed' of God, in a special sense of the word—the king of the future. Isaiah 9^{1-6} and 11^{1-9}, passages of the greatest significance for all succeeding time, are the brilliant stars whose gleam prefigures that expectation. There are some investigators by whom these passages are not assigned to Isaiah. In any case we must go back as far as the later exilic time; but hitherto no really decisive proof has been brought forward. The birth of such a hope in the time of Isaiah is quite intelligible. During the decline and subsequent fall of the dynasty of David the Jewish people could not forget the pristine glory of that house. They clung to the promise which had been given to David, 'Thine house and thy kingdom shall be made sure for ever before thee; thy throne shall be established for ever.'[1] And so, about the ruins of the fallen tabernacle of David, the hope crept and climbed that once again a king of David's house should come, victorious, mighty, as in the old time, but also a ruler after God's heart, under whom peace reigns in the land and righteousness prevails. The figure of the Messiah is therefore connected in the closest way with the national expectation of the people, with the overthrow of their enemies, with his own powerful lordship. The dominant influence of these conceptions continued to operate in the piety of the people.

Still, the idea of the Messiah was not without its history. Just in the last centuries before Jesus it fell much into the background, as the conviction

[1] II Sam. 7^{16}.

gained sway that God himself, by a miraculous interposition from heaven, would effect a radical revolution in all the relations of the world; in one department of Jewish literature indeed—as we shall see in the next chapter—the Messianic idea itself underwent a fundamental transformation. There were times, such as the glorious period of the Maccabean dynasty, when people believed they were already living in the Messianic era, that the Messiah was already before them in the person of the reigning prince; times in which king and priest were one. The best known witness of this is Psalm 110.[1] But when the Maccabees fell a quick revulsion came to pass in the popular feeling. The Maccabees were now the blasphemers, who had arrogantly usurped the kingly dignity; the hope for a coming Messianic king, which had never been extinguished, even in times for which we have no testimony, was now again fanned to a bright glow. This is nowhere so clearly to be seen as in the Psalms of Solomon, already often mentioned; their high-strung expectation gives us our most important witness concerning the popular Messianic conceptions in

[1] Cf. also the Testament of Levi, 18.

the last decade before Jesus. That a strong Messianic excitement was stirring among the people at the time of Jesus' appearance is certain. This is proved by such a figure as that of John the Baptist, the state of mind of Jesus' disciples, the expectancy of the crowds, and the pretenders to the office of Messiah from among the Zealots, who continued to appear, down to Barkochba in Trajan's time.

If we now ask, more in detail, what the nature of the Messianic conceptions were when Jesus appeared, we must emphasize strongly at the outset that in the whole of Judaism, down to Jesus' time, no trace of a suffering Messiah is to be found. If Jesus held that in spite of his sufferings, in spite even of his shameful end, he himself it was whom God should send as Messiah, that was an act of his own, personal, valiant faith. It was not until much later that Judaism began to speak of a suffering Messiah, and it then contrived to remain faithful to its original view by distinguishing between two Messiahs—a dying Messiah, the son of Joseph, and a victorious lord, the son of David. In Jesus' time the expected Messiah was to be a triumphant ruler over Palestine and the Jewish people, whose sway should inaugurate the new age. In accordance with Malachi 3^{1} Elijah was looked for as his forerunner.[1] Moses and Enoch had also been regarded as precursors. Since Isaiah 11^{1} it had been held as an unshakable certainty that the Messiah must be a descendant of David.[2] As regards his relation to God it was by no means the case that God was in any way eclipsed by the Messiah. On the contrary he is the gift of God's grace, he 'whom God has chosen,' he appears at the time 'which thou hast chosen, O God, that he may rule over thy servant Israel.'[3] It is God's faithfulness, compassion, grace that permits the son of David to arise; God's glory is reflected in him.[4] The seventeenth of the Psalms of Solomon begins and closes with the words, 'The Lord (God) is our King for ever and ever.' But in truth there does exist a close, personal relation between God and Messiah, though always a relation in which the Messiah is subordinate. He is directed by God; he lives in the fear of God; God is his king, his hope; God gives him his spirit, his wisdom,

[1] Jesus Sirach 48^{4} and ^{10}; Mark 6^{15}, 8^{28}, 9^{11} sq., 15^{35} sq.

[2] E.g. Ps. of Solomon 17^{21}; Mark 12^{35}, 10^{47}; Rom. 1^{3}; II Tim. 2^{8}, and many other passages.

[3] Ps. of Solomon 17^{21}, ^{42}.

[4] Ps. of Solomon 17^{3} sq. ^{21}, ^{31}

his strength.[1] All this is expressed compactly in the phrase—not, however, a very frequent phrase—'Son of God,' which refers to Psalm 2^{7}, understood in a Messianic sense.[2] But what is intended by this title is certainly only an inner, personal, spiritual relation between God and Messiah, not a physical relation, transcending the spiritual. His nearness to God comes out in the character of the Messiah. He is energetic, upright, wise, filled with the spirit; he will not stumble, he is even sinless.[3] Whenever the moral qualities of the Messiah are depicted the influence of Isaiah 11^{1-9} is quite especially prominent. Yet again, it is his abundant endowment with the spirit which explains that expectation, revealed in the New Testament, of special miracles to be wrought by the Messiah.[4] But however clearly we must recognize that Jewish piety ascribes to the Messiah a high level, indeed a unique level of religious and moral worth, which is described sometimes in glorious words, yet in the mind of

1 Ps. of Solomon $17^{32, 34, 37-40}$.

2 In the New Testament, e.g., Mark 3^{11}, 5^{7}.

3 Ps. of Solomon 17^{36}; Testament of Levi 18. For the application of this Messianic dogma to Jesus in the New Testament, cf. II Cor. 5^{21}; Heb. 4^{15}, 7^{26}; I Pet. 2^{22}; I John 3^{5}.

4 Matt. 11^{2-6}, 12^{38}.

the Jew, when he thinks of the future son of David, what stands first is something else—the overthrow of enemies, the glorious kingly rule in Palestine. This brings us to the last point, the fate of other nations in the Messianic age.

That same seventeenth Psalm of Solomon, upon which I have already drawn considerably for illustration, begins its picture of the glorious future (cf. 21-25) in quite different tones. How characteristic these verses are! Yes, it was of this that every pious Jew of that time thought first, when he spoke of the Messiah—the shattering of enemies with a staff of iron, destruction of the Roman empire, which had now laid its heavy hand on the Holy Land as once, in Daniel's time, the Grecian empire had done. Jewish piety is filled with that thirst for revenge to which this is a religious desire—'In thy lovingkindness cut off mine enemies, and destroy all that oppress me, for I am thy servant,'[1] which could apostrophise Babylon, 'Happy shall he be that seizes and dashes thy little ones against the rock.'[2] Psalm 2⁹ and Isaiah 11⁴ were especially favourite passages. The Messiah, Yahweh, and his angel play

[1] Ps. 143¹². [2] Ps. 137⁹.

here the same part. The Jews themselves too are sometimes thought of as sharing in the work of retribution.[1] It is in the valley of Jehoshaphat by Jerusalem that the great judgment of destruction shall go on.[2] The frightful description in Joel 3^{16}, 'Yahweh roars from Zion, and utters his voice from Jerusalem, that the heavens and the earth shake,' had given wide scope to passionate dreams of revenge. This can be clearly traced in Revelation 14^{20}, where, in a passage originally Jewish, a slaughter so hideous is looked for that the blood reaches to the bridles of the horses, a thousand six hundred furlongs wide.[3] Those Gentiles who do not fall victims to destruction—for here the representations vary: sometimes all perish, sometimes only the oppressors—serve only as vassals to exhibit the triumph of the Jewish people in its full glory. They do not form an object of independent interest; they are not to be won by teaching and conversion; but they may bring their treasures, and foreign kings may count it an honour to serve Jerusalem, as Isaiah 60^{1-17} had described so clearly and decisively for all

[1] Thus Enoch 90^{19}.

[3] Cf. Enoch 100^{1-3}.

[2] Sometimes an actual conflict is thought of; more often a divine judgment, carried out, perhaps, by fire.

the time to come.[1] At most the Gentile nations shall receive the leaves of the tree of life, while its fruits are reserved for Israel.[2] But Palestine and Jerusalem will then be 'pure,' free from all gentile defilement. Thus Joel had already prophesied, 'Jerusalem shall be holy, and strangers shall no more pass through it.'[3] And it resounds again in the Psalms of Solomon that the Messiah shall distribute the holy people over the land according to their tribes, 'and neither aliens nor strangers shall dwell among them any more.'[4] That is the ideal. In this point the exclusive, strictly national character of this piety is especially palpable. And yet there were, connected with these national hopes, feelings of another kind, strongly individualistic, such as appear in the expectation of the resurrection and retribution in a future world. But they can better be dealt with in the next chapter, in connexion with that peculiar manifestation which we are accustomed to call the Jewish Apocalyptic. For we then learn to conceive resurrection and future retribution not as isolated, extraordinary forms of belief, but as necessary constituents of a new and complete theory of the world.

[1] Rev. 21^{24}. [2] Rev. 22^{2}. [3] Joel 3^{17}. [4] 17^{28}.

CHAPTER IV

THE JEWISH APOCALYPTIC

THE phenomena which we have now to discuss cannot well be brought under the head of popular piety, for we are here dealing only in part with a common possession of the great masses. Those national aspirations which we have just considered were really a common possession. We learn from the New Testament that even the disciples of Jesus clung to them to the last. This is shown by the petitions of the sons of Zebedee,[1] and by the utter lack of understanding which the disciples showed in view of Jesus' path of suffering. It speaks in Luke 24^{21} and Acts 1^{6}. But this new range of thought does not stand in any opposition either to the popular or the Pharisaic religion. There were apocalypses which clearly betray the Pharisaic standpoint, even though most of them did not

[1] Mark 10^{37}.

originate in the circles of the scribes, but in those of the laity; and on the other hand the views of these remarkable writings were represented far and wide among the people, to some extent indeed had reached the stage of general conviction, as in the case of the doctrines of resurrection and retribution. The newer, individualistic piety of the Church stamped itself strongly upon these works, while nationalistic traits are not lacking. It is also incorrect to regard the apocalyptic literature as a sort of heretical backwater of the legal Judaism, though Jewish scholars are apt to take this view. In the writings themselves there is no trace of anything of the kind. The volume of this literature, and the fact that the Christians simply took over the Jewish apocalypses, and wrote similar works themselves, tells strongly against such a notion. It was not until after 70 A.D., when the school of the Talmud, the strictly legal, rabbinical school had gained the day, that the apocalyptic literature was rejected. But at this point it is necessary to go farther back, and make clear the real nature of this phenomenon.

We are not dealing with a few isolated writings, but with a widely ramified literature, which, as the name Apocalypse, 'Revelation,' implies, professes to reveal something. This something was nothing less than the divine secrets, which would otherwise have been hidden from mankind. The first apocalyptic book which we know is actually in the Old Testament canon; this is the book of Daniel, written in the year 165 B.C. Its most important successors down to the time of Jesus' ministry are the book of Enoch, preserved in the Ethiopic language; the Jewish writing which is the basis of the Testament of the Twelve Patriarchs; the third book of the Sibylline Oracles; the Ascension of Moses; perhaps too the 'Slavonic' Enoch. But the fourth book of Ezra and the Syriac Apocalypse of Baruch, which belong to the end of the first century and are among the most remarkable of the Jewish apocalypses, must also be considered.[1] Among the Christian Apocalypses, which made great use of Jewish material, and are written in just the same style and tone, we must mention, besides the Revelation of John

[1] See Appendix. All the works mentioned except the Slavonic Enoch are to be found in a German translation in Kantsch, 'die Pseudepigraphen des Alten Testaments,' 1900. [The greatest authority on this subject in English is Dr. R. H. Charles, whose article in the Encyclopædia Biblica is an admirable introduction to the Apocalyptic Literature.]

which stands in the New Testament, the Revelation of Peter, the Shepherd of Hermas, the Ascension of Isaiah, the fifth and sixth books of Ezra, and the Christian Sibyllines.[1]

If we ask, first of all, what are the marks of this literature in respect of form, we at once encounter a remarkable interweaving of revelation and concealment. The secret of God, which has been hidden from eternity, is indeed to be revealed, but not for every one; it is again concealed, though not so utterly as to make a revelation impossible. A light, transparent veil is thrown over the matter, to screen it from rude, intrusive eyes, while the understanding soul, guided by the spirit, is able to see through. Thus in Daniel the name of Antiochus Epiphanes, in the Revelation of John the name of Nero, is never uttered; the one speaks of the 'little horn,' the other of the 'beast,' but the reader of that age with any insight knew quite well what was meant. The word, 'He that hath ears, let him hear,'[2] is here especially applicable. 'Teach it to the wise among

[1] All published in German in Hennecke's 'Neutestamentliche Apokryphen,' 1904. [For the English literature in this field see Dr. Charles's article in the Encyclopædia Biblica.]

[2] Revelation of John 13[9].

thy people, of whom thou art assured that their hearts can grasp and hold thy secrets'; so we read in IV Ezra 12^{38}.[1] 'Thou revealest not thy secrets to the great crowd,' writes the Syriac Baruch 48^{3}. In these passages the consciousness of the apocalyptic writers speaks very plainly, and we clearly recognize that their piety cannot simply be equated, without further ado, with that of the great multitude. In order to understand this peculiar combination of revelation and concealment we must keep in mind that the Apocalypses were produced in times of bitter strife. Plain speaking, at such times, means setting life at stake. Daniel predicts, as a seer, the downfall of the hated reign of the Seleucidæ, while Antiochus IV (Epiphanes) holds Palestine in his power. The authors of IV Ezra, the Syriac Baruch, and the Revelation of John beheld their deadly foe in the Roman Empire, but were nevertheless its subjects. But besides this political motive there was a religious motive—the feeling that the divine secrets can never be made perfectly intelligible to terrestrial man. 'For as the land is given over to the forest and the sea to its waves, even

[1] Cf. Eph. 1^{14}.

so can the dwellers upon earth know nothing but the earthly, and only the celestials can know what is in the heights of heaven.'[1] Man cannot fully understand the ways of the Highest: 'But thou, a mortal man, that livest in the transitory aeon,[2] how canst thou conceive the eternal?'[3] This religious thought colours the presentation of the whole revelation, which, in its very secretiveness, evinces its supernatural character, its celestial origin. Often, of course, half the mystification is mere literary mannerism.

Another formal mark of this literature is closely connected with the preceding: the whole of it is pseudonymous. The concealment of the writer is quite in keeping with that of the revelation. Here too, however, the veil is generally thin enough. Every reader with any skill in history can easily see that the writers do not belong to the age to which they profess to belong. This again was due to the stress of the times. On the other hand it beseemed the divine revelation to choose the noblest organs for its utterance. The authors do not venture to come forward in their

[1] IV Ezra 4^{21}. [2] Aeon,—age in the world's destiny.
[3] IV Ezra 4^{11}.

own insignificant person ; they call up the grand forms of a hoary antiquity, such as Enoch and Moses, or of epoch-making periods, such as Ezra and Baruch, men of whom we may read in the Old Testament, as we do of Moses, that God spake with them face to face, or, as of Enoch and Elijah, that God withdrew them to himself. It seemed natural and credible enough that such men as these should receive a mysterious, divine revelation. This is another case in which it would be quite out of place and unhistorical to regard pseudonymity simply as a literary fraud. The authors were certainly convinced that the great beings under whose names they put forward their writings had long been in possession of all these revelations. At the same time it cannot be denied that the mere instinct of literary imitation also played a part, especially in later times.

Finally we must take note that the whole apocalyptic is, as regards its form, soothsaying, chiefly in the way of visions. We certainly do find, side by side with this, certain speculations, which strike us to-day as highly bizarre, concerning the secrets of the universe—speculations chiefly of an astronomical kind—but beyond question the chief interest of the writers lies in the future. The divine mysteries have yet to be revealed. All those frequent retrospects over the historical past, which begin if possible with the beginning of the world, are never the result of a mere historian's interest in anything which used to exist; they serve only as pointers into the still unknown future, which shall lead to the unveiling of the mysteries of God. And since celestial things can never be quite adequately represented, it is necessary to employ as illustration figures which, nevertheless, have always the effect of partly concealing what they would exhibit.

If we turn from form to matter, the first impression we gain from the whole apocalyptic is that of the strange, grotesque, fantastic. The reader, for instance, who comes in the Revelation of John upon the woman arrayed with the sun, and the moon under her feet, and upon her head a crown of twelve stars, or the great red dragon, that cast the third part of the stars to earth with his tail, or the beast with ten horns and seven heads, or finds in the Slavonic and the Ethiopic Enoch the most extraordinary descriptions of a series of heavens and their contents, stands in face of something utterly unintelligible, a book with seven seals. It is only when we pay heed to the numerous allusions to contemporary history, and especially when we consider this whole material in its relation to the wider history of religion, that light breaks on our darkness. The apocalyptic consists partly of very ancient, sacred, mythological elements from foreign religions, which have migrated from people to people, and are often misunderstood or reinterpreted by the author himself, but, in our eyes, only really begin to live when they have been brought back into their original setting—so to say, brought home again. This is the starting-point, and a very important field of labour, in the modern researches of Protestant theologians in the history of religion.

If we regard the piety of the apocalyptists, we easily perceive an intense, but at the same time overstrained and therefore morbid religiosity. The source from which the apocalyptic draws its religious power is an unconquerable conviction that it stands at the end of this world. It flows through these works like a broad river: the end is near, very near. 'The aeon hastens mightily towards its end.'[1] The past stands to the short remaining time as a rain-storm to a single drop, as a huge fire to a last wisp of smoke. 'The youth of the world is past, and the vigour of creation has long come to an end, and the coming of the time is all but here, and nearly overpast.'[2] It is these apocalypses, indeed, which most eminently represent the new belief of the church, that God will reveal himself in the future. In the numerous passages which might here be cited religious power is really found. Face to face with evil, man clings to God and his heaven, and yearns ardently for his coming. What a deep influence such a feeling could have is shown especially by IV Ezra and the Syriac Baruch, where the terrors of the divine judgment rise up before even the pious man, and the penetrating sense of his own sin grows up beside that of the general sinfulness of his race. The conviction that the end of the world is imminent fans religious fervour into flame; the soul alienates itself from the world and turns with all its energy to God. This is, then, beyond question, a mighty religious power, which reveals its force most strongly in

[1] IV Ezra 4^{26}. [2] Syr. Baruch 85^{10}.

Jesus and in primitive Christianity. If Jesus was saturated with the sense that he had come in the last hour before the shutting of the door, if he was convinced that there were people belonging to his own generation who would not die, but would see the end of the world,[1] if as a result all else sank to nothing in his eyes compared with the saving of the soul out of the firebrand of this world, in all this he was, beyond doubt, under the influence of the apocalyptic. And yet, in the apocalyptists, this religious tension overstrains itself, and becomes irreligious. Man is able to calculate the end of the world. This point is of supreme importance to our understanding of the apocalyptic. The conviction that the end is near leads to the question, how long will it be till then? The underlying thought is this: 'God has weighed the aeon in the balance, he has measured the hours with a measure and counted the times by number. He disturbs them not and wakes them not until the measure ordained be fulfilled.'[2] But then comes the inevitable moment. 'The Highest looked upon his times, and lo, they were at an end, and his aeons, lo, they were full.'[3]

[1] Mark 9^1. [2] IV Ezra 4^{36} sq. [3] IV Ezra 11^{44}.

But if God has fixed a definite measure for the times of the world, then the soul illuminated by God's spirit, initiated into his secrets, can reckon them up; and so this arithmetic, this assumption of exact knowledge, pervades the whole apocalyptic. Daniel takes up Jeremiah's prophecy of the seventy years and interprets it as meaning seventy weeks of years, after which the end of the world is to come. According to the Ethiopic Enoch the duration of the world amounts to ten thousand years, according to the Ascension of Moses twenty thousand. It is therefore easy to understand that in the apocalyptic figures play a very considerable part. The most important phenomena are brought forward in the guise of numerical values. Numerical riddles are propounded.[1] At this point mystery turns to mystification. Piety takes a morbid direction, and becomes at bottom irreligious; it lacks the calm, equable trust in God, which can await his good pleasure. The Lord of heaven is dictated to; curiosity, the hankering after superterrestrial knowledge, carries things with a high hand. It is exceedingly significant that in this matter Jesus

[1] Cf. Revelation of John 13^{18}.

has not followed the apocalyptic. His intimate religious communion with God was involuntarily offended by it. Moreover Jesus himself perceived and expressed his opposition to it: 'Concerning that day and the hour none knoweth, not even the angels of heaven, not even the Son, but only the Father.'[1] The apocalyptic itch for calculation is always felt by the truly religious man as a usurpation of the rights of God.[2] We must also observe that calculation is not only to be found where definite figures are given; the exact exposition of a series of premonitory signs in strict succession belongs to the same field; it is indirect calculation.

If we compare the apocalypses with the older Jewish views, even those of the earlier post-exilic period, the most important difference that confronts us is the dualism of the apocalyptic theory of the world.[3] It is the most decisive characteristic of this class of literature, a new trait, foreign to Judaism. Two ages of the world confront each other in irreconcilable contrast,

[1] Matt. 24^{36}. Cf. Luke 17^{20}.

[2] Cf. e.g., Luther's distaste for the Apocalypse.

[3] Dualism means the setting up in opposition to each other of two, and only two, irreconcilable principles.

'this age' and 'the age to come,' the present and the future aeon. The present world is bad, the prey of Satan and the demons, given over to irremediable destruction. The future world is utterly different, good, divine, eternal. Here the expectation of the future is purely supernatural. Everything earthly must first fall to final ruin, and then comes something altogether new. It cannot be put more clearly than in IV Ezra 4^{27} sqq. 'This aeon is full of mourning and hardship. For the evil concerning which thou askest me is sown, and its harvest has not yet appeared. So long then as that which is sown has not yet been reaped and the place of evil seed has not yet vanished, the field, where the good is sown, cannot appear.' It is by no means merely a question of the destruction of evil, but also of the disappearance of the earth as the place of evil seed. A new, good field will appear. The future world has long existed in heaven, created by God before the creation of the world.[1] The extraordinary significance of these new views does not consist merely in the substitution of a heavenly hope for an earthly, but chiefly in the possibility which they

[1] Cf. Syr. Baruch 51^{8}; IV Ezra 8^{52}.

establish of breaking down utterly that national narrowness in religion which we recognized so clearly in the preceding chapter. The outlook becomes world-wide. What is concerned is no longer merely Palestine and its destiny, the future of the Jewish people. Worlds confront each other and wrestle together. God and Devil, angels and demons wage battle. Who does not know how Jesus, in line with this view, conceived of his whole ministry as a warfare against the kingdom of Satan and his evil spirits ?[1] Jesus' general theory of the world is derived from the apocalyptic, and is but a temporary husk for the eternal religious and moral truth which he brought. It was in the domain of these views that the religious individualism which, as we have seen, arose and spread also in the legalistic, churchly piety, attained its most effective power, even though it never reached a definite formulation. Still this field shows very real preparatory steps towards the gospel of Jesus, as we shall at once recognize if we now deal briefly with details. In this examination we can attempt to establish the main

[1] Mark 3^{22-27}; Matt. 12^{28}. All Jesus' healings of demoniacs should be considered from this point of view.

features. Precisely in the apocalyptic there is such a wealth of heterogeneous material that this limitation is absolutely necessary.

That the present world is bad is a fundamental conviction in this literature. The world stands under the influence, partly indeed under the lordship, of evil spirits. The belief in dark powers, demons, and the like, was in Jesus' time quite general.

No doubt there always existed in the Jewish religion, as in all popular religions, and even in the prophetic period, a belief in evil, uncanny spectres, and goblins. What is new in the apocalyptic is the remarkable prominence of this belief, and the consolidation of all these beings to a kingdom of evil under a monarchical government. A Satan is certainly known to the Old Testament; but he is an angel by the throne of God, whose duty it is to discharge the functions of accuser—an office which he uses, it must be admitted, with malicious arrières pensées. This Satan, who also bears the names Mastema, Beliar, Beelzebub, has become in the apocalyptic what naïve popular belief even yet understands by the word 'devil'—God's antipodes, the ruler in the realm of evil. Under him come the demons, the offspring of those sons of God whose offence is recorded in Genesis 6^2; these, as fallen angels, seduce man to evil, especially to idolatry, in invisible forms stir up the vilest passions, and engender all possible diseases.[1] They dislike to stay in their proper habitation, the desert, but in countless numbers they surround mankind, and lie in wait to destroy him. Thus did later Judaism behold this world, and there can be no doubt that Jesus simply inherited and shared these views. Jesus wages warfare against Satan and his kingdom. In his age these were no metaphors for the power of evil, but perfectly real and very terrible entities.

A world which had given itself up to these dark powers must come to destruction. But the nearer this destruction draws, the more frenzied become the efforts of the realm of Satan. He even emerges from his invisibility; he becomes human in the Antichrist, the last diabolical birth before the end, who is sometimes endowed with the features of a tyrant,[2] sometimes with those of a

[1] Job 1 and 2; Zech. 3; I and II Chronicles.

[2] With a reminiscence of Daniel's portrait of Antiochus Epiphanes.

false prophet.[1] The most remarkable witnesses to the expectation of Antichrist in the New Testament are II Thess. 2^{1-12} and Revelation of John 13. Then, when God prepares to intervene, mankind will know it by the 'woes of Messiah.' Failures of harvest, unheard-of natural portents, especially signs in heaven, bodily degeneration in the human race, appalling confusion among the nations, war in the family, all against all, the incursion of terrible, mysterious peoples, among whom, in consequence of Ezekiel 38 sq., Gog and Magog are the most renowned—these are the woes. They announce the day of divine judgment which is then to dawn, the day of judgment for the world, to which all will be subjected, a day on which the dead arise. This resurrection of the dead, which is for the most part realistically conceived as a bodily rising, is one of the most important new views of late Judaism. It exhibits with especial clearness the supersession of the national idea, and the assertion of the individual as such. Ancient Israel had known nothing of any resurrection from the dead. Death ended all. The soul passed into

[1] In reminiscence of the third book of the Jewish Sibylline Oracles.

the Sheol, Hades, the realm of shadows, of which the Psalmist sings, 'In the Sheol who shall give thee thanks?'[1] The new hope first meets us in Isaiah 24–27, in that interpolation well called the apocalypse of Isaiah, and written towards the end of the third century B.C.: 'Awake and sing, ye that lie in the dust, for thy dew is a dew of the light, and the earth shall cast forth the shades.'[2] Then in Daniel we read the celebrated passage: 'Many of those that sleep in the dust of the earth shall awake, some to everlasting life, and some to shame and everlasting contempt. But the wise shall shine as the brightness of the firmament, and they that have turned many to righteousness as the stars for ever and ever.'[3] It is well worthy of attention that here many, and not all, are said to rise. The writer is thinking especially of the martyrs. Even Luke 14^{14} speaks only of a resurrection of the righteous. It is in the Ethiopic Enoch that we first find the general resurrection of the dead,[4] which is formulated by IV Ezra as follows: 'The earth gives back them that rest within, the dust releases them that sleep in it, the chambers restore again the souls that were

[1] Ps. 6^5. [2] Is. 26^{19}. [3] Dan. 12^2. [4] 51^1, 61^5.

entrusted to them.'[1] This article of belief, which was derided by so late a book as Ecclesiastes,[2] was acknowledged, at the time of Jesus' ministry, by all the pious. Jesus himself accepted and sanctioned it.[3] Paul treats it as self-evident,[4] though not in the solid, corporal sense of the popular imagination. The extraordinary, indeed inestimable significance of this belief lies in the supreme importance of the individual person; his actions and omissions make all the difference. The whole Jewish scheme which was concerned only with this life is finally superseded. This is very clearly seen in the manner in which the great day of Yahweh is now conceived. Once it was the longed-for day on which Yahweh is to take vengeance on the foes of his people, exert his old nature as a god of battle in bloody slaughter, and let Israel triumph; and now it has become the day of the judgment of the world. All men that ever lived must appear before the throne of God and receive sentence according to their works—a purely juridical act. Daniel gives a magnificent metaphorical description: 'I gazed on till thrones were placed, and one with many days sat down;

1 7^{32}. 2 3^{19-22}. 3 Mark 12^{18-27}. 4 I Cor. 15^{12} sq.

his raiment was white as snow, and the hair of his head pure as wool; his throne was of fiery flames, and had wheels of burning fire. A fiery stream flowed out far and wide before him. Thousand thousands served him, and ten thousand times ten thousand stood at his bidding. The court sat, and the books were opened.'[1] In the judgment, which goes on to its end amid mighty catastrophes of nature, these books play a momentous part. The names or the deeds of men stand written in them. There is, as we have seen, a special heavenly secretary, Michael.[2] The book of life, too, is occasionally mentioned separately. In this court takes place the final decision of the lot of a man. After exact weighing of his works he either enters into eternal life or goes to eternal damnation. It is the works that decide. This constitutes the link with legalistic piety. That it is in reality the state of a man's spirit which finally turns the beam is a profound truth that remained completely hidden from Judaism, and was first set upon the candlestick by Jesus. But it is palpable that in the eyes of this apocalyptic, with its world-wide outlook, it was no longer member-

[1] Dan. 7^9 sq. [2] Enoch too frequently receives this office.

ship of the Jewish people but individual piety that really mattered. Religious individualism has here won the victory over the national religion, even though at the same time certain nationalistic elements still held their ground with ineradicable tenacity. This is and remains, in spite of all that is fantastic in its detailed conceptions, the immeasurable significance of this apocalyptic speculation. It prepared the way for the word of Jesus, 'What does it help a man if he win the whole world and lose his own soul?'[1] And this idea of divine retribution for every individual in the future life casts its shadow before upon the time between death and resurrection to judgment. The old conceptions of Sheol were more and more transformed. In the intermediate time there is a foretaste of the fate to come. The souls of the pious come into pleasant, lucid regions of the underworld; they can already behold their future blessedness; or they are preserved in subterranean chambers, in deep peace, under the care of angels; sometimes they are even already in heaven.[2] On the other hand the souls of the ungodly go down to cold and dark places, are

[1] Matt. 16^{26}. [2] Luke 16^{23}.

forced to wander without rest, and are already tormented.[1] The final retribution after the judgment is thus potent beforehand. Incidentally it should be noted that in Alexandrian Judaism, and also occasionally in that of Palestine, the final retribution follows immediately after death. The soul of the pious man comes at once to God; that of the ungodly is at once annihilated. Here, too, Greek ideas, Platonic ideas, have often exerted an influence; but we cannot now enter into detail. In the main stream of Palestinian Judaism it is always after the resurrection, in the divine judgment, that the human soul is overtaken by its final destiny. And in what does this consist? First of all the pious receive eternal life. They enter upon a new, supernatural, intransient existence in the divine glory. Light and life are here very closely allied.[2] It is extremely clear that this new life was nevertheless contemplated in earthly colours. Man cannot escape from the images of the life that surrounds him; his thought is bounded by earthly forms. The Jewish people certainly formed very sensuous, realistic conceptions of the life eternal, as indeed

[1] Luke 16^{23}. [2] Dan. 12^{3} sq. Ethiop. Enoch 58^{3}.

often happens even in our own day, and must always continue to happen. The pious enter into the Paradise, the Garden of Eden transferred to heaven; this garden, in which according to the legend Adam dwelt, is now said to have existed before all creation. There they lead a joyous being by the tree of life, whose fruits, which confer immortality, they enjoy, and by the water of life, which they may now drink. Connected with this is the idea of a heavenly Jerusalem, which is the old, earthly Jerusalem transferred to heaven, and is now depicted in the most radiant colours.[1] That is the glorious fate of the pious. And the ungodly? They go into eternal damnation. Darkness and destruction are here closely allied. They are tortured or annihilated. Fire plays a great part in these conceptions. The terrible and hideous vision of hell takes form. While according to the older view the enemies of Israel were to be destroyed with pain in the valley of Jehoshaphat, now the impious are to be tortured for ever in a subterranean or celestial place of torment, a fiery furnace or a lake of fire. These are the two different fates which follow upon the universal

[1] Revelation of John 21.

judgment, with which the present, terrestrial world passes away; the mode of its passing is sometimes taken to be a vast conflagration. And then the new heaven and the new earth, which were once spoken of figuratively in Isaiah 65^{17}, come in complete reality, the second, supernatural, divine world of the good. This was the resplendent image offered to hope by the apocalyptic writers, an image which is, however—inevitably, as we have seen—depicted in earthly colours. It so comes to pass that we often find in their descriptions a grotesque mixture of concrete earthliness with the celestial and the supernatural, so that at the first glance we may well doubt whether we are still amid the pictures of the old or already in the new. But taken as a whole there is no possible doubt that the apocalyptic makes a decisive, thoroughgoing cleavage between this life and the next; it represents a dualistic theory of the universe. And what has become of the Messiah? Within the frame of this picture he seems to have no place. In fact there is a series of apocalypses which do not mention him at all.[1] But where he does appear he has become quite another being.

[1] E.g., Daniel, and the Ascension of Moses.

We may even speak of a new, a second Messianic figure, so great is the transformation. The son of David, the ideal of a theocratic king, who rules over the Jewish people in Palestine with justice and righteousness, has become a heavenly, spiritual being, who existed with God before the creation of the world,[1] and remained safe in his presence, to emerge and descend at the end of the age upon the clouds of heaven, surrounded by angels. His title runs: the Son of Man. The most remarkable fact is this, that the new figure of Messiah shows no trace of a gradual development, but starts into being in a moment, like Athene from the head of Zeus. We find it in the imagery of the Ethiopic Enoch, especially chapters 46–49,[2] and again in IV Ezra 13^{1-13}, $^{25-51}$. There is a tendency to connect it with the celebrated passage in Daniel, 7^{13} sq.: 'I saw in the night visions, and lo there came one like unto a son of man, and he came to him of many days, and they brought him near before him. And there was given him dominion and honour and lordship, that all peoples, nations, and languages should serve

[1] The 'pre-existence' of Messiah.

[2] Consider more particularly 48^{2-6}, 49^{2}.

him. His rule shall be everlasting and shall not pass away, and his kingdom shall not be destroyed.' But neither the new conception of Messiah nor the title Son of Man has its origin in this passage. Apart from the fact that Daniel is certainly not speaking of the Messiah, but of the people of Israel—though on this point his later readers might easily fall into a misapprehension—the figure of this son of man in this context in Daniel is itself a riddle, which calls for explanation. It is most probable that we have here the influences of foreign religions, though we are certainly not able to point them out exactly. Most of the apocalyptic writers desired to retain the Messiah. But the earthly ruler was no longer applicable; so he was united with a divine, spiritual being, who must have possessed the prototype of human form; he too was transferred to heaven, in conformity with the supernatural character of the apocalyptic. That this new heavenly Messiah is a patched-up compromise, who would be better away, is easily seen in the uncertainty of the writers regarding his function. In Enoch 48^4 sq. we read: 'He will be a staff for the righteous and holy, that they may lean on him and not fall; he will be the light of the people and the hope of those that are troubled in heart. All that dwell upon the mainland will fall down before him and adore and give praise, laud and extol the name of the lord of spirits. To this end was he chosen.' How indefinite all this is, and what is the use of it? According to IV Ezra he shall redeem creation, create the new order of things, destroy the army of the nations that bands itself against him, and protect united Israel.[1] Here we can detect a much stronger echoing of the old ideas of Messiah. A much greater advance is made when this celestial figure is actually appointed by God to be the judge of the world.[2] It is of course true even here that the new image of the Messiah nowhere appears quite unadulterated, but is considerably alloyed with old characteristics—indeed, that can be seen quite clearly in the Revelation of John—but that does not affect the fact that in reality there are two different pictures. The desire to combine the old picture with the new has led to the peculiar doctrine of an intermediate Messianic kingdom.

[1] IV Ezra $13^{26, 34-38, 49}$.

[2] Eth. Enoch 51, 55, 61–63; cf. Matt. 25^{31-46}.

Before the general resurrection and the great judgment Messiah shall reign with the righteous upon earth. The duration of this kingdom is variously given. The reign of a thousand years, the millennium,[1] has become especially celebrated through the Revelation of John 20⁶, and has often played a momentous part in the history of the church. But what gives the newer image of Messiah its highest significance is the fact that the Messianic consciousness of Jesus was founded upon it. The old idea of Messiah could not possibly, in view of the whole nature of Jesus, be adopted by him. But the new idea opened out to him the possibility of connecting his unique religious consciousness of sonship and vocation with the highest title that Judaism possessed. Jesus then believed, not that he was the Messiah (in the old national sense) but that he would become the Messiah (in the new apocalyptic sense), that he would come as Messiah upon the clouds of heaven.[2]

It used to be a favourite device to associate

[1] Chiliasmus, or Millenarianism.

[2] See, for a more detailed exposition, Bousset: 'Jesus,' Chapter III.

the apocalyptic with Israelite prophecy. But the apocalyptists themselves do not claim to be prophets.[1] Prophecy is extinguished, and they are the wise men, privileged above the crowd, to whom the secrets of God have been confided. In fact, then, and in spite of a few lines of connexion,[2] the difference is really profound. The visions alone are enough to make this clear. The prophets had real visions, inner experiences which convulsed the soul, the forms of which they transferred, with great agitation, to the world of reality outside them. If this transference, this imputation of external reality was illusion, still the inner experiences were intensely real. The creative power of God worked in them from time to time with compulsion, with enormous, original force, often against their own human thoughts and opinions. It is not to be denied that the apocalyptists may also have had such actual visions[3]; but the vision is certainly in their case

[1] The Revelation of John, enveloped as it is in the Christian consciousness, forms a not unintelligible exception.

[2] We meet these especially in Joel 3 and in IV Ezra I and Zechariah.

[3] There are even signs to be observed that the Rabbis of the first century A.D. were themselves not without ecstatic experiences.

for the most part a mere form of literary art. They write in the visionary style, just as we may write in the style of the fairy tale. The imitative instinct which was so characteristic of the apocalyptic comes clearly to light in this use of the prophetic ecstasy. The artificial character of most apocalyptic visions reveals itself—apart altogether from their great number—especially in the fact that it is quite impossible to unite them into one consistent spectacle. We are presented with an abundance of the most heterogeneous and often impossible details. The extraordinarily complicated, elaborate, and unnatural character of these visions points to the play of a rankly luxuriant imagination. If, for instance, the Revelation of John be read from this point of view, the proofs will present themselves in superflux. The vaticination, too, of the prophets and of the apocalyptists is different. What the prophets aim at is the clear understanding of their own contemporary conditions; the whole interest of the apocalyptists lies in the future. The prophets are men who enter passionately into the great questions and contests of their time, but, filled with the spirit of Yahweh, will not let themselves be dazzled by externals; taught by the past they have gained a genuine insight into historical events, and are so able to show a right estimate of the future. On the other hand the apocalyptists despair of the world altogether. Past and present are so bad that one can only learn from them that this world must needs fall a prey to destruction, and a new, good world come in its place. What the apocalyptic aims at is to gain a conception, here and now, of that future world, and above all to know when it is to come. And accordingly it does not give us prediction, but uncontrollable speculation bound up with divination: for the apocalyptic calculation of coming events is nothing else. And how different is the kind of future which the prophets and the apocalyptists contemplate! The prophets are predominantly concerned with the future which stands connected with the present. Even when they think of a more distant future, and however much they may transform and idealize, it still remains always terrestrial, within the sphere of national expectation. On the contrary the apocalyptists are concerned with a future which shall arrive through an utter breach with the present—the new, celestial aeon, which is utterly different from the world that now is. The dualism of their world-theory is the unbridgeable chasm which separates apocalyptic from prophecy. Prophecy knows no such dualism, and, consistently with this, knows nothing of the resurrection of the dead, the universal judgment, paradise and hell; the whole detail in the two settings forth of the future is different; and, as we have seen, the Messianic hopes had to undergo a complete transformation.

The question, then, forces itself most strongly upon us, what is the source of all this new element in the apocalypses; above all the new dualistic theory, the great dramatic fight to an end between the kingdom of Satan and the kingdom of God, ending in the universal judgment, with all its accompanying phenomena and its consequences? It cannot be denied, when this is compared with the earlier Israelite religion, that something new is here to be seen. We may remind ourselves that in the earlier time even evil was occasionally associated with Yahweh[1]; that in the prophets evil arises in the will of man, in his disobedience, his perversity, but no trace is to be found of any

[1] II Sam. 24[1].

Satanic realm of evil. We might be tempted to derive the new matter in the apocalyptic from Daniel. It is certainly evident that the whole of the later apocalyptic takes its stand on this work, and dependence upon it cannot be denied. Must we then regard the author of Daniel as an eminent creative personality, whom the later writers have merely imitated? The work itself, however, certainly gives us no such impression. I have already pointed out, while considering the new Messianic idea in the apocalyptic, that a close consideration of this book impresses us with the conviction that Daniel, too, was working with traditional materials, which do not consistently cohere. This is, indeed, the case when we consider the writing in other aspects; and so the question at once arises, whence did Daniel obtain the new element? It is not without justification that an appeal is made to the severe oppression of the Maccabean age, under which, in this book of Daniel, the first apocalypse meets us. Much may be explained by reference to this, especially for instance the eager expectation of a speedy end, the judgment. That time under Antiochus Epiphanes was so terrible that we can understand how such a yearning could arise. We might perhaps also assume that the fate of the righteous, who suffered a martyr's death, wrung the hearts of pious men, and called forth the hope that they would not be allowed to remain in death; God must, for his righteousness' sake, awaken them unto life. But even here all that is really comprehensible is that an already existent belief in the resurrection should have been laid hold of, and not that such a belief could have been actually engendered by the desire of certain individuals. Above all, the rise of a theory of the world which was at once dualistic and individualistic, such as that in which this belief in the resurrection was firmly planted, cannot be regarded as a necessary or even intelligible outcome of the confusion of those times. It is remarkable that the figure of the heavenly Messiah is first found in the Ethiopic Enoch, long after the time of terror was past. No external origin in an historical situation can be established. There is only one possibility left to explain the new element, namely that foreign religions have exerted an influence on later Judaism. First and foremost we might consider the Persian religion, with which Judaism came into contact in the Babylonian plain. The Babylonian empire was superseded by the Persian. We should remember the friendly relation in which Judaism stood to this very Persian power. Cyrus permitted the Jews to return from Babylon ; in the second Isaiah he is even denoted as the Messiah. In other matters, too, the Persians showed kindness towards the Jews. It is therefore not difficult to conceive that religious elements might have penetrated into Judaism from a Persian source. And in this Persian religion, which likewise possesses its apocalyptic, we find what we need. Dualism was its own, ancient, original belief. Ahura-Mazda (Ormuzd), the supreme good God, and Angra-Mainyu (Ahriman), the evil spirit, had always confronted one another in sharp antagonism. The whole history of the world is a varying contest between these two powers, which ends with a decisive victory of the good God. Here we have the two worlds—the old world is at last destroyed with fire—the general judgment, the resurrection of the dead to be judged, the terrible torture of sinners. Indeed all that we seek is here to be found, at least the essential, dualism and world-encompassing speculation. It must not be denied for a moment, it is rather to be expected from the first, that there are differences, some of which are important, between Persian and Jewish apocalyptic. Nobody maintains that the Persian apocalyptic was taken over wholesale, lock, stock, and barrel. But we may hold that at decisive points Persian influences were operative. Besides the Persian religion those of Babylon and Egypt seem also to have affected Judaism, which had likewise come into close contact with them both. There are numerous points at which that can be shown with great certainty. In the region, for instance, of the doctrine of angels and demons we come across conceptions which, while they are unintelligible as purely Jewish products, are at once explained by a glance at the Babylonian religion. We cannot here pursue this subject into detail. It must always be remembered that we are dealing with the period of world-wide Hellenistic civilization, the great age of the mixture of religions. From the time of Alexander the Great the different peoples mingled like rushing waters, and with them their ideas and their religions. In spite of the mighty reaction of the Maccabean age Judaism was no longer able to hold itself aloof. On the contrary we observe in all fields that late Judaism exhibits specifically the character of a mixed religion.

CONCLUSION

If we now look back once more over the region which we have traversed, in order to realize as a whole the religious tone and temper of the Judaism of that time, our soul stands face to face with a remarkable scene, which we contemplate with mixed feelings. With what fervour, yea, with what passion, did this unique people long for the living God! Who can read the never-ageing Psalms without feeling, 'Here is genuine religious feeling at its source; here is also true religion'? There is no other people which even approaches the importance for religion of the Jews. Paul was well warranted in testifying of his own nation that they had a zeal for God.[1] And yet a misguided zeal, which found no true satisfaction. We have made acquaintance with the whole gamut of human feeling, from the most tremulous anguish

[1] Rom. 10².

of a profound sense of sin to a man's most arrogant confidence in his own performance. Alongside the individual piety stood the strong tenacity of the nationalistic religion, beside the life lived in the present stood the life lived in the future, beside the spirit of penance stood the spirit of triumph. And between them, all the many various shades of feeling. We see a heaving and tossing, out of which now this mood emerges, now that. But one thing we miss, the unshakable rock in the raging sea, the unity in multiplicity, the sure peace amid the tumult. He who surveys the whole must say, after all, Judaism lacked that stability of confidence which is certain of the issue. Where one day the most emphatic confidence was ostensibly felt the next day might see the most painful insecurity. At the time of the appearance of Jesus the Jewish religion oscillated dubiously between extremes. There was no certainty of salvation.

Amid this flux and reflux of the most various religious moods Jesus appeared, and wrought, for all his dependence upon the conceptions of his age and the surroundings under which he grew to manhood, a complete change of value in the decisive, fundamental factors. The Jew had a high opinion, when all was said, of his own person and the worth of his own performance. Jesus, on the contrary, has taught all ages the unforgettable lesson that when the single man has done all that it was his duty to do, he is an unprofitable servant.[1] Jesus has destroyed the religious worth of single performances as such, and—in spite of all his diligent insistence on active goodness—pointed to the fountain of a truly good and heartfelt intent as the really momentous thing. On the other hand the Jewish thought of God was intrinsically mean, for he was conceived in the image of a strict taskmaster. Jesus, on the contrary, has taught all ages unforgettably his immeasurably grand conception of God, which culminates in the saying that one sinner who repents is of more value in his eyes than ninety-nine righteous persons, who need no repentance.[2] In its deepest sense he set upon the candlestick that word, 'A man sees what is before his eyes, but the Lord looks upon the heart.'[3] What Jesus brought could not but be felt, and was felt indeed, as a wonderful message of joy, whose words fell

[1] Luke 17^10. [2] Luke 15^7. [3] I Sam. 16^7.

like sunshine into the hearts of all th
and were heavy laden,[1] all those that, b
the crushing load of the single legal ordinances, could neither attain to true earthly energy nor to true communion with God. Jesus gave the great and needful liberation from all religious frittering and futility. He set man straightway before God himself, but before the face of a Father, bringing us at once a mighty obligation and a mighty enfranchisement. Thereupon the whole confusing multiplicity of individual works passed out of thought; Jesus brought rest to the soul, the only true and certain peace of a heart made one with God.

[1] Matt. 11[28].

APPENDIX

I. Historical Table from the Exile to the Destruction of Jerusalem.

This longer period is chosen because the stage of development in which the Jewish religion stood at the time of Jesus' ministry began with the Exile and ended with the destruction of Jerusalem. It was not until after 70 A.D. that complete legalistic ossification, with elimination of the popular piety and the apocalyptic, set in—the supremacy of the Rabbis. Only the most important dates are here given.

B.C.	
586–538	The Jews in exile in Babylonia.
538	Cyrus, king of the Persians, puts an end to the Babylonian empire and permits the Jews to return. First return of the exiles under Zerubbabel and Joshua.
538–332	Palestine under Persian suzerainty (from Cyrus to Darius III).
458	Return of a second body of exiles under Ezra.
445	Nehemiah governor in Jerusalem.
444	The Law is published by Ezra: probably not the whole five 'books of Moses,' but chiefly one of the sources of these books, namely, the so-called Priestly Codex. Pledging of the people to keep the Law.
332	Alexander the Great destroys the Persian empire, and so gains sovereignty over the Jews.
332–320	Palestine under Macedonian governors.
320	Capture of Jerusalem by the Egyptian king Ptolemy I, Lagi.

B.C.	
320–197	Palestine alternately under Egyptian and Syrian rule.
301–264	Happy time of peace under the mild government of the Egyptian dynasty of the Ptolemies.
197–167	Palestine under the Syrian rule of the Seleucids.
175–164	Antiochus IV, Epiphanes, king of the Syrians.
175–168	Forcible Hellenising of the Jews by Antiochus Epiphanes. Attempt to destroy the Jewish religion. Profanation of the Temple.
167–142	The Jewish war of liberation under the leadership of the Maccabees (the priests Mattathias and his sons Judas, Jonathan, Simon) against the Syrians.
165	New consecration of the Temple.
142	Recognition of the independence of Judæa by the Syrian king Demetrius.
141	The Maccabees or Hasmonæans (so called from their ancestor Hasmon) are by popular decision recognized as the high-priestly and princely dynasty.
141–63	Palestine under the rule of the Hasmonæan dynasty (Simon, John Hyrcanus, Aristobulus I, Alexander Jannæus, Alexandra, Aristobulus II).
63	Pompey takes Jerusalem. From this point onwards continuous Roman rule.
37 B.C.–44 A.D.	Frequently interrupted rule of the Idumæan family of the Herods in Palestine as a whole or parts of it, under Roman suzerainty.
37 B.C.–4 B.C.	Herod the Great.
4 B.C.–39 A.D.	Herod Antipas ruler over Galilee and Peræa: Jesus' sovereign.
A.D.	
27–36	Pontius Pilate procurator of Judæa.
about 29	Public appearance of Jesus. } During the reign of the Roman Emperor Tiberius, 14-37.
about 30	Death of Jesus. }
66–73	The great fight against Rome.
70	Destruction of Jerusalem by Titus.

II. Chronological Survey of the most important Literary Sources.

B.C.	
about 180	The Wisdom of Jesus Sirach, a voluminous collection of sayings, written originally in Hebrew, with the object of showing how a happy life can be led in practical wisdom. (About 130 translated into Greek by the grandson of the author.)
165	The Old Testament book of Daniel, the first apocalypse.
about 140	Close of the Old Testament collection of Psalms. The songs belong altogether to the post-exilic time. Many are of late date.
about 140	The third book of the Sibylline Oracles, a kind of Alexandrine apocalypse, which contains little of religious value.
about 140	The book of Esther relates in the form of a novel, with passionate hatred against foreigners, the origin of the feast of Purim, and has likewise found a place in the Old Testament.
about 130	The Jewish writing underlying the Testament of the Twelve Patriarchs (in the time of Hyrcanus). Admonitions, given before death by the twelve sons of Jacob to their children, concerning jealousy, envy, chastity, arrogance, courage, etc. The writing, as we now have it, contains Christian interpolations.
about 130-100	The chief constituent part of the Ethiopic Enoch, an important apocalypse. The figurative discourses, chapters 37–71, belong to the years 104–78 and are not of Christian, but like the rest of Jewish origin.
about 130–70	The book of Judith, a legend, written from the Pharisaic point of view, of the murder of the general Holophernes, who was in the service of Nebuchadnezzar, by Judith.

B.C.	
about 100–63	The first book of the Maccabees, in the main an excellent, credible account of the Maccabean revolt.
about 70	The book of Jubilees or the Little Genesis, a haggadic commentary on Genesis (time of Alexandra).
63–48	The Psalms of Solomon, written from the Pharisaic point of view, with a strong emphasis on the Messianic hope.
(?)	The book of Tobit, a novel-like account of the fortunes of a pious Jew, which was written during the last 200 years B.C., in any case before the beginning of the Herodian Temple in 21 B.C.
(?)	The second book of the Maccabees, an unhistorical account, written in an edifying vein, especially of the time of Judas Maccabæus; Pharisaic tone; actually an attack on the Maccabees.
(?)	The Wisdom of Solomon, one of the most important writings of Alexandrian Judaism, which was written between Sirach and Philo, probably nearer to the time of Philo.
4 B.C.–6 A.D.	The Ascension of Moses, a fragment of an apocalypse, in which Moses gives his successor Joshua a revelation concerning future events till the end of the world; probably not by a Zealot, but by a pious man who set himself against all sanctimonious hypocrisy.
A.D.	
about 20	The literary work of the Alexandrian Philo.
(?)	In the first century: the fourth book of the Maccabees, an edifying philosophical sermon on the command of the passions by the reason, guided by the Law; of Alexandrian origin.
(?)	The Slavonic Enoch, in the first half of the first century, certainly before 70 A.D., clearly shows the combination of Judaism with Platonic, Parsi, Egyptian, and Babylonian elements.

A.D.

76–79 The work of the Jewish historian Josephus 'on the Jewish War.'

93–94 Josephus' Jewish Archæology (Antiquities).

about 81–96 IV Ezra, the most important Jewish apocalypse, whose object is to comfort the Jews, driven almost to despair by the destruction of Jerusalem, with the nearness of the new aeon and its solution of all riddles.

about 100 The Syriac apocalypse of Baruch, with the same object as IV Ezra, and no doubt written later.

about 50–150 The writings united in the New Testament. Among these the genuine words of Jesus, the old sources of the Gospels and Acts, the letters of Paul, written by a whilom Pharisee, and the Revelation of John (which has made considerable use of originally Jewish material) offer a rich field of material for the understanding of later Judaism.

All the sources here named, so far as they are not contained in the Old or the New Testament, with exception of the Slavonic Enoch and the works of Philo and Josephus, are accessible to every reader of German in the work of E. Kantsch, 'Die Apokryphen und die Pseudepigraphen des Alten Testaments,' 2 vols., 1900.

Protestant and Jewish scholars differ in their use of sources to this extent, that in depicting the Judaism of Jesus' time the protestants prefer the above named contemporary sources, while the Jews pay more regard to later sources. Among these should be mentioned the Mishna (doctrine) and Tosephta (completion, i.e., of the Mishna), in which the customary law was reduced to writing. The Mishna received its final redaction at the end of the second Christian century. The Talmud, both the Palestinian (belonging to the fourth century A.D.) and the Babylonian (the sixth century), is a detailed commentary on the text of the Mishna, with edifying as well as legal matter. The Targums are Aramaic, often free paraphrastic translations of the Old Testament text, dating from the third and fourth centuries A.D. The Midrashes contain commentaries on the text of scripture, especially the later, edifying kind; they begin with the second century A.D. These writings contain very much older material, especially the Mishna, and the tract Pirke Aboth, i.e., Sayings of the Fathers, utterances of certain renowned teachers, mostly of the period 70–170 A.D., but also of earlier date. (This tract is embodied in the Mishna, but does not belong to it). The preference of contemporary sources is justified: (1) because it is a general methodic principle to adduce the literature which stands nearest in point of time; (2) because after 70 A.D. a considerable change befell Judaism in the direction of legalistic rigidity; (3) because the older material of the later rabbinical literature can only be employed after a very difficult, critical sifting, and in accordance with views which can be substantiated by means of contemporary sources.

III. Survey of the most important Literary Sources, classified with regard to their contents.

A.—Palestinian Literature.

1. Historical works: I Maccabees, Josephus.
2. Proverbial literature: Jesus Sirach, Pirke Aboth.
3. Religious poetry: The latest Old Testament Psalms, the Psalms of Solomon.
4. Edifying legends: Esther, Judith, Tobit, II Maccabees.
5. Haggadic interpretation: Jubilees.
6. Apocalypses: Daniel, Testament of the Twelve Patriarchs (original basis), Ethiopic Enoch, Ascension of Moses, Slavonic Enoch, IV Ezra, Syriac apocalypse of Baruch.

B.—Alexandrian Literature.

The Sibylline Oracles, Wisdom of Solomon, the writings of Philo, IV Maccabees.

LITERATURE

Among important scientific works the following deal with this subject :—

*Schürer : 'Geschichte des jüdischen Volkes im Zeitalter Jesu Christi,' 3 vols., 3rd ed., 1898–1901.

Bousset : 'Die Religion des Judentums im neutestamentlichen Zeitalter,' 1903.

On the Jewish side the most important work is :—

*Graetz : 'Geschichte der Juden,' 4th ed. 1888.

These works are helpful for scholarly study. The general reader may consult :—

Wellhausen : 'Israelitische und jüdische Geschichte,' 4th ed., 1901.

Schlatter : 'Israels Geschichte von Alexander dem Grossen bis Hadrian,' 1901.

O. Holtzmann : 'Die jüdische Schriftgelehrsamkeit zur Zeit Jesu,' 1901.

Bousset : 'Die jüdische Apocalyptik,' 1903.

Baldensperger : 'Das spätere Judentum als Vorstufe des Christentums,' 1900.

The three last named are shorter expositions.

* English Translations :—

Schürer : 'A History of the Jewish People in the Time of Jesus Christ,' 5 vols., 1890 (translated from the second German edition).

Graetz : 'History of the Jews,' 5 vols., 1891–2.

Verzeichnis der erschienenen Volksbücher.

I. Reihe: **Die Religion des Neuen Testaments.** 1. Wernle: Die Quellen des Lebens Jesu. 11.—20. Taus.—2./3. Bousset: Jesus. 21.—30. Taus.—4. Vischer: Die Paulusbriefe.—5./6. Wrede: Paulus. 11.—20. Taus.—7. Hollmann: Welche Religion hatten die Juden als Jesus auftrat?—8. u. 10. Schmiedel: Das vierte Evangelium gegenüber den drei ersten.—12. Ders.: Evangelium, Briefe und Offenbarung des Johannes.—9. v. Dobschütz: Das apostolische Zeitalter.—11. Holtzmann: Die Entstehung des Neuen Testaments.—13. Knopf: Die Zukunftshoffnungen des Urchristentums.—14. Jülicher: Paulus und Jesus.—15. Geffcken: Christliche Apokryphen.—16. Brückner: Der sterbende und auferstehende Gottheiland i.d. oriental. Religionen u. i. Verhältnis z. Christent.—17. E. Petersen: Die wunderbare Geburt des Heilandes. 1909.—18./19. Weiss: Christus. Die Anfänge des Dogmas. 1909.

II. Reihe: **Die Religion des Alten Testaments.** 1. Lehmann-Haupt: Israels Geschicke im Rahmen der Weltgeschichte. (In Vorbereitung.)—2. Küchler: Hebräische Volkskunde.—3. I und II. Merx: Die Bücher Moses und Josua.—5. Budde: Das prophetische Schrifttum.—7. Beer: Saul, David, Salomo.—8. Gunkel: Elias.—9. Nowack: Amos und Hosea.—10. Guthe: Jesaia.—14. Löhr: Seelenkämpfe und Glaubensnöte vor 2000 Jahren.—15. Benzinger: Wie wurden die Juden das Volk des Gesetzes?—17. Bertholet: Daniel und die griechische Gefahr.

III. Reihe: **Allgemeine Religionsgeschichte. Religionsvergleichung.** 1. Pfleiderer: Vorbereitung des Christentums in der griechischen Philosophie.—2. Bertholet: Seelenwanderung—3. Söderblom: Die Religionen der Erde.—4. Hackmann: Der Ursprung des Buddhismus.—5. Ders.: Der südliche Buddhismus.—7. Ders.: Der Buddhismus in China usw.—6. Wendland, Die Schöpfung der Welt.—8. Becker: Christentum und Islam.—9. Vollmer: Vom Lesen und Deuten heiliger Schriften.—10. Gressmann: Die Ausgrabungen in Palästina u. d. A. T.

IV. Reihe: **Kirchengeschichte.** 1. Jüngst: Pietisten.—2. Wernle: Paulus Gerhardt.—3./4. Krüger: Das Papsttum. Seine Idee und ihre Träger.—5. Weinel: Die urchristliche und die heutige Mission.—6. Mehlhorn: Die Blütezeit der deutschen Mystik.—7. Holl: Der Modernismus.—8. Ohle: Der Hexenwahn.—9. Baur: Johann Calvin. 1909.

V. Reihe: **Weltanschauung und Religionsphilosophie.** 1. Niebergall: Welches ist der beste Religion?—2. Traub: Die Wunder im Neuen Testament. 11.—20. Taus.—3. J. Petersen: Naturforschung und Glaube. 11.—15. Taus.—4. Meyer: Was uns Jesus heute ist.—5. O. Schmiedel: Richard Wagners religiöse Weltanschauung.—6. Bousset: Unser Gottesglaube.

www.ingramcontent.com/pod-product-compliance
Lightning Source LLC
LaVergne TN
LVHW021410110826
845150LV00007B/1859

* 9 7 8 1 4 2 5 5 7 2 1 7 4 *